Glacial Hills Review

Summer 2024

Nonfiction, Poetry, Art

Chocofpleirn Press

i

Glacial Hills Review

Summer 2024
Art, Nonfiction, Poetry

Copyright 2024

Choeofpleirn Press Editors
James P. Cooper, Art & Poetry
Ruth J. Heflin, Art & Nonfiction

Choeofpleirn Press is a small, private press publishing literary journals in northeastern Kansas at the foot of the Glacial Hills. Our goal is to promote the best written and photographed creations we can in each magazine and book we publish.

We publish four separate journals a year: *Coneflower Café* (Spring), *Glacial Hills Review* (Summer), *Rushing Thru the Dark* (Autumn), and the *Best of Choeofpleirn Press* annual (Winter). The Spring, Summer, and Autumn journals are each dedicated to one of three major genres of storytelling: short fiction, nonfiction, and drama respectively. The first place winners and finalists of the five creative contests held by CP—the Derick Burleson Poetry Prize, the Ben Nyberg Short Fiction Award, the Phil Heldrich NonFiction Award, the Susan Hansell Drama Prize, and the Mary Cassatt Art Award—are republished in the Winter *Best of Choeofpleirn Press* magazine. The first place award in each category comes with a cash prize.

Readers can purchase individual digital issues of each magazine as ebooks directly through our website. As ebooks (pdf), individual issues cost $6 each; annual digital subscriptions cost $24.

Readers who prefer print copies can purchase individual magazines from Amazon. These print copies make excellent coffee table books because they are a full 8.5"x11" in size and printed in full color on quality paper.

Writers and other literary presses can also purchase classified or photo ads to appear in specific magazines in an effort to promote their own works or websites. See our website, www.choeofpleirnpress.com, for details and the back of this magazine for examples.

Contact Choeofpleirn Press through choeofpleirnpress@gmail.com.

ISSN: 2769-0105 (digital) 2769-0083 (print)
ISBN: 979-8-9904058-5-1 (print) 979-8-9904058-6-8 (digital)

Cover photo by Jennifer Weigel, "Spiders from Mars"

Editors' Note

We started Choeofpleirn Press in the autumn of 2020, after having been sidelined from teaching our college classes by the pandemic. Ruth had long wanted James to sign on to beginning our own literary press, and, with time on our hands, we decided there would never be another opportunity like that one to pool our decades of working for other literary magazines to good use.

However, we both had stipulations. Ruth, having worked as support staff for the esteemed *Kansas Quarterly* for years, knew that one thing we did not have was space for storing volumes of unsold magazines, so we decided that everything we produced had to be either digital or sold online only.

Ruth—who has explored more writing genres than James, the dedicated poet, has—also wanted to include publications of one-act plays and short screenplays, since most of the literary magazines in America studiously ignore drama for various bigoted reasons. One New York City literary employee told us, once, that drama had its own support system, something poetry and fiction do not. Maybe that is true in NYC, but not in Kansas.

We began by deciding to publish four annual literary magazines, with the hope that we could gain enough income from the 5 creative contest fees and subscriptions, not to mention online magazine sales, to sustain the press.

We quickly realized in 2021, however, that there just aren't enough hungry writers and artists willing to pay contest fees out there, and most readers our age prefer print magazines, not digital ones.

So we had to correct course, and filed for nonprofit status—an exceedingly frustrating process that took more than a year to accomplish—in order to apply for grants to support the press, since we were mostly supporting the press through our limited retirement savings. We have yet to have this effort rewarded with a grant, since so many granters seem to have a similar attitude toward a literary press in the "middle of nowhere" Kansas that the lit mag employee above does—we just are not significant enough or live in a state that is important enough to bother with.

We also added two book contests to the roster, hoping the small "royalty" (usually less than $1) we could gain from publishing books through online platforms would help support the press.

However, after three years of being denied grants, we find ourselves at a familiar precipice for many literary publishers in America today.

Despite our innovations to literary magazines—producing large 8x11.5" magazines ablaze with color and great literature, all while never having to store print copies to sell—and despite the wonderful poetry and nonfiction books we have published, despite expensive efforts to advertise through magazines like *Poets & Writers*, despite online advertising of our books and magazines on social media—we find our press is struggling severely to stay financially afloat.

That said, if we do not receive any funding from the 2 grants we have applied for this year, we will have to stop publishing literary magazines like this one in 2025, since Ruth will have to obtain paying income again.

As a precaution, we advise all of our contributors to buy a physical copy of the magazines in which they appear from their favorite online bookstore in order to have a copy of your work for the future. We have lost track of the number of writers who have contacted us, asking us to republish a work they had published previously in a now defunct literary magazine because they never bothered to buy a physical copy of that magazine.

Buy your copies now. Before it's too late.

At the very least, please support Choeofpleirn Press by following us on Facebook and X (formerly Twitter).

As always, we appreciate our loyal contributors and donors. Without you, we are nothing.

Choeofpleirn Press Supporters

We wish to thank the following donors for their generous support of our press:

Christine Andersen

Karyn Bruce

Joseph Cappello

G.W. Clift

Jeffrey Feingold

Louise Kantro

Madeline Wise

Tracy Robert

and several donors who wish to remain anonymous.

Contents

Art

Jennifer Weigel	Spiders from Mars	cover
Donna D. Vitucci	Highrise	2
Donna D. Vitucci	Foxtails	14
Gregory Stump	Asemic Text w285	22
Gregory Stump	Asemic Text w338	29
Gregory Stump	Asemic Text 2347	49
Tammy Higgins	The Eyes That See	59
Andrew Graber	Pastel Pastiche	67
James P. Cooper	Chasing a High, Lawrence, Kansas	73
Izzy Lippincott	Sunrise over a Kansas Field	81
Izzy Lippincott	Kansas Ziggurats	88
Andrew Graber	Leaves on Water	97
Izzy Lippincott	Papercut Sunflower	102
James P. Cooper	VA Abandoned Stairs	123
James P. Cooper	Lake Jeanette	130
Izzy Lippincott	Super Cell, Pratt, Kansas	136
Izzy Lippincott	Double Rainbow, Pratt, Kansas	144

Essays

Jeffrey Utzinger	Undusted Still	3
Karen Colstrom	A Kansas Photographer's Inspiration	16
Enda M. Brennan	A View of the Interstate	24
Jenn Dean	The Supermodels	31
Katrina Irene Gould	Going All In	51
Sylvia Sensiper	About Face	61
Becca Bullen	Beauty Is Pain	69
Debra Solomon Baker	Molting	75
Mark Lewandowski	On Bilbo	83
Wayne Glausser	My Father's War	90
Glenn Moss	Ebbets Field Bounce	99
Michael Milburn	Slights	105
Sara R. Sands	Christmas in Dubai, 2011	125
Dawn Colclasure	My Emotional Escape Space	132
Jennifer Weigel	Reversals Artworks: Reflecting Upon My Art Process	138

Poetry

Craig Kirchner	Late Night	1
Dave Malone	Burnt Bones of Our Home	13
Caryn Mirriam-Goldberg	Empty Nest	15
Caryn Mirriam-Goldberg	Apricots	21
Caryn Mirriam-Goldberg	Covid When Daylight Savings Time Kicks In	23
Victoria James	A ~~Poet~~ (Mom) Delivers Her Own Eulogy	28
Victoria James	Motherhood on 11x17 Canvas, Mixed Media	30
Angela Waldie	On the Wing	48
Angela Waldie	Feathers and Catkins	50
John Grey	October Twilight	58
LindaAnn LoSchiavo	Cedar Waxwings in the Hospital's Playground	60
Buff Whitman-Bradley	Why Do We Always Get Lost?	66

Joel Robbins   The Artist   68
Kurt Cline   The Great Highway   72
Kurt Cline   Sun Ra   74
Joan Penn   Carousel Ride   80
Andrea Reynolds   Where Dreams Take Place   82
Steven Pelcman   Luxembourg Gardens, Paris   87
William Derge   Japanese Beetle Trap   89
Steve Brisendine   This'll Be the Day   96
Miriam Manglani   Lucid Dreaming   98
Leah Wenger   Healing: Half-Forgotten   101
Amaka Chime   Voiceover   103
Linda M. Crate   You Fell   122
B.P. Mihalich   Portrait in Sepia   124
Craig Kirchner   A Ceiling He Didn't Know   129
Craig Kirchner   Thank God   131
Noah Hubbell   It All Begins in Water   135
Chris Litsey   Terrible Heart Rate   137

Contributors' Notes   145
Ads   150

Alpha List of Contributors

Debra Solomon Baker 75
Steve Brisendine 96
Becca Bullen 69
Enda M. Brennan 24
Amaka Chime 103
Kurt Cline 72, 74
Dawn Colclasure 132
Karen Colstrom 16
James P. Cooper 73, 123, 130
Linda M. Crate 122
Jenn Dean 31
William Derge 89
Wayne Glausser 90
Andrew (Andy) Graber 67, 97
Katrina Irene Gould 51
John Grey 58
Tammy Higgins 59
Noah Hubbell 135
Victoria James 28, 30
Craig Kirchner 1, 129, 131
Mark Lewandowski 83
Izzy Lippincott 81, 88, 102, 136, 144
Chris Litsey 137
LindaAnn LoSchiavo 60
Dave Malone 13
Miriam Manglani 98
Brittney Pierce Mihalich 124
Michael Milburn 105
Caryn Mirriam-Goldberg 15, 21, 23
Glenn Moss 99
Steven Pelcman 87
Joan Penn 80
Andrea Reynolds 82
Joel Robbins 68
Sara R. Sands 125
Sylvia Sensiper 61
Gregory Stump 22, 29, 49
Jeffrey Utzinger 3
Donna D. Vitucci 2, 14
Angela Waldie 48, 50
Jennifer Weigel cover, 138
Buff Whitman-Bradley 66
Leah Wenger 101

Late Night

Craig Kirchner

Insomnia and I decide to get up
and check out some late-night TV.
It's a mutual decision, but he gets credit for the idea.
I'm going to have a coffee, hazelnut,
and he's down with the 12-year-old bourbon, neat.

He just couldn't get comfortable,
and I was struggling with the bad knees.
He tells me I should get them replaced,
compares them to the week-old bread on the counter,
and the dishwasher that just went up.

We very seldom see eye to eye,
perhaps because he's often hard to look at.
I wanted to watch a Ken Burns documentary,
he's pushing for a Soprano's binge,
something that could keep us up for days.

I beat him at Gin, but I think he lets me.
He loves when we think of something to write about,
always suggests we scribble, then rewrite.
He never seems to have any ideas or input,
says it's not his job to interfere.

When we lay back down, he gets creative,
We need to discuss the big moments,
relive the details as best we can,
and he justifies that strategy by explaining,
We've been here for over 40 million moments.

When we're ready to call it a day,
we need to play those top two dozen oldies,
keep putting quarters in the juke until
we get through all the greatest hits,
start with that blonde in the eighth grade.

When up, I need to start getting him to help out.
If he can't suggest a line or a metaphor,
he could empty that new dishwasher he's impressed with,
do a load of laundry. If I could talk him into walking the dog,
I might be able to get back to sleep.

Highrise

Donna D. Vitucci

Undusted Still

Jeffrey Utzinger

While tidying his cabin by Walden Pond, Henry David Thoreau developed what I call "the limestone test"—a method for determining how serious you are about simplifying your life. Thoreau writes: "I had three pieces of limestone on my desk, but I was terrified to find that they required to be dusted daily, when the furniture of my mind was all undusted still." The word "terrified" here might seem overkill to some; however, it suggests the slightest misstep, even in housekeeping, could derail Thoreau's two-year experiment. Allowing clutter to gather on his writing desk, and dust to settle on the clutter, all while in pursuit of a minimalist lifestyle, causes him to throw the limestone "out the window in disgust." *Disgust*. Terror and disgust at extraneous objects in one's writing space is an austerity to which I can only aspire.

I can also only imagine the disgust with which Thoreau would regard the ceramic figurine in his likeness that sits on my writing desk (next to statuettes of Lincoln and Melville, and frightening stacks of papers and books. Terrifying layers of dust.). Thoreau's head is removable, and inside you'll find a pale blue circle ringed with green ersatz foliage. Behold: Walden Pond in miniature.

The first time my wife, Christa, and I made the pilgrimage to Concord during our honeymoon, nearly thirty years ago, I was shocked (yes, *shocked*) by the size of Walden Pond. After we snapped pictures posing next to Thoreau's statue, and we peeked into the cabin replica, descended the path that leads to the water, and emerged from the trees, I couldn't process what I was seeing. In Northern Kentucky where I spent my childhood, we called "ponds" the little watering holes that cows drink from while you fish for bluegill, trying not to cast too far lest bait and hook reach the opposite bank and tangle in a clump of weeds. Walden Pond, in my estimation, was a *lake*. And there were people swimming in it. Rowing canoes. It was all too big. Too busy. *Do these people even know*, I wondered with disgust, *what a sacred space this is?*

Reading *Walden* the first time, as a high school senior languishing in the Ft. Worth suburbs, was a similarly disorienting experience. Our teacher had provided no context suspecting, I suppose, that we would all read a summary version, which after an hour or so of fumbling through the strange text, is exactly what I did. That copy of *Cliffs Notes on Thoreau's Walden* is probably serving as silverfish fodder somewhere in my boxed childhood, housed beneath holiday decorations in the garage. However, I have a vivid memory of reading an explication of a moment from "The Ponds" in which Thoreau writes, "Walden is blue at one time and green at another, even from the same point of view." I don't recall, exactly, how the metaphor was spun—something like green and blue represent Thoreau's malleable emotional state—but I received a profound sense of double calling that afternoon: I wanted to be the type of person who writes about the minutiae of the natural world, *and* I wanted to figure out how one becomes a person who explains the meaning of texts. Who was this Cliff guy, and how did he know what he knew about what Henry David Thoreau was thinking when he wrote about the color of water?

In college, I bought a copy of *The Modern Library*'s *Walden and Other Writings of Henry David Thoreau* and, despite my deep admiration for Thoreau and his book, I was scarcely better at close reading after earning an English degree than I was as a high school student cutting corners. I failed to notice that shortly before Thoreau waxes about the multi-colored iris that is Walden Pond, he mentions he's "spent the hours of midnight fishing from a boat by moonlight . . . anchored in *forty feet of water*." I should have been prepared for the watercraft speckling the surface of the lake-sized Walden Pond.

Nonetheless, Christa and I walked the pond's perimeter, followed the path through the woods to the spot where the cabin once stood, saw the cairn, retraced our steps to find a stone so I could leave my own offering, and then headed for the Shop at Walden Pond. Among the coffee table books, t-shirts and caps, inspirational quotes suitable for framing, I encountered blueprints for building your very own Thoreau cabin replica. The prints are based on research conducted in the 1940s by Roland Wells, an amateur archeologist and historian. While I didn't doubt the veracity of Mr. Wells' work, I balked at the cost of the blueprints mass produced from his findings: fifty dollars.

"Thoreau spent just over twenty-eight bucks using mostly recycled material to build the cabin," I told Christa as we stood admiring the blueprints.

"You should get *something*," she said.

"Buying a *Simplify, Simplify, Simplify* coffee mug that you don't need or house plans you'll never use doesn't quite capture the spirit of Thoreau," I said.

I left the gift shop empty handed and smug.

My self-satisfaction dissipated once we drove a few miles to visit the Thoreau Special Collections at the Concord Free Public Library where we encountered a man with unkempt hair, wearing an ill-fitting sports jacket, whom I suppose was a librarian. I don't recall him introducing himself, only his abrupt: "what questions do you have?"

Christa and I were the only other people in the small room dedicated to Thoreau's collection, but the curator motioned for us to sit, pulled up a chair a few feet in front of us, and demanded a second time to know the purpose of our journey.

"He's the one who's read it, not me," Christa said, poking me gently with her elbow. The only question I could think of us was *why do they call it a 'pond' when clearly it's a lake?*, but I could sense whatever scorn this Thoreau librarian had for our lack of insightful questions might turn to rage if I asked something that stupid.

"I don't think I have any questions," I stammered.

"What can you tell us?" Christa asked.

"Everything," he snorted. "But I can't tell you *anything* until you ask me *something*."

I felt as though we had fallen down the rabbit hole, or that perhaps this man was actually a Thoreau reenactor rather than a librarian, and he'd decided that Thoreau was indeed a misanthrope. Or perhaps he suspected I'd been taught Thoreau took his dirty clothes home to his mother on weekends and sat by his parents' hearth to warm himself with fire and food when the New England nights grew too cold. Somehow, he knew I'd only skimmed the surface, that my introduction to *Walden* was through *Cliffs Notes*, that I already regretted not buying a *The Mass of Men Lead Lives of Quiet Desperation* t-shirt.

I don't recall how Christa and I extricated ourselves from our interrogator, but I probably mustered some inane question, and we left the Concord Free Library in search of less demanding experiences like shopping for handmade pottery, cups and bowls in blue and white speckled patterns—things that probably would need dusting when not in use (and, all these years later, I can attest that they do).

I have questions now, good questions (I think) but ones that have taken shape only after thirty years of living with my battered *Modern Library Walden*, reading it every five years or so, highlighting or underlining passages in different colors to mark what seems significant during another season of my life. At some point, I wrote my name on the flyleaf along with this note to myself: "Keep this book forever, and read it often."

I have thought deeply about this text, and I do have questions, ones that revolve around Thoreau's blind spots, namely: why couldn't Thoreau see that the repeated use of the word, "savage" to refer to Native Americans was unacceptable? The easy answer is, of course, that it's complicated, that the word was used by nineteenth-century, white writers so frequently as to not warrant mention. People have written entire books on Thoreau's interest in the Indigenous people of New England. At the risk of oversimplifying the conversation, the consensus among some readers of Thoreau's work is that when it comes to Native Americans, Thoreau's heart was in the right place; his language was in the wrong.

For me, the savage/civilized dichotomy that runs throughout *Walden* is *the* central part of the shameful history of settler colonialism and American Indians, and so it's difficult to see past the language. And yet, in his own idiosyncratic way, Thoreau makes the case that the supposed "savage" Penobscot Indians, the Indigenous people he knew best, had figured out how to avoid a trap that many white Americans never did (or do): home mortgages. In "Economy," Thoreau writes: "It is evident that the savage owns his shelter because it costs so little, while the civilized man hires his commonly because he cannot afford to own it." Thoreau points out the illogic of someone working ten to fifteen years to pay off a home mortgage, and as someone who started a fifteen-year mortgage then rolled it into a twenty-year mortgage to buy a nicer home, and then refinanced that mortgage to afford even more square footage, and still has seven years to go before (presumably) ever actually "owning" a home, I can appreciate Thoreau's point. Summing up his discussion of housing costs, Thoreau asks a good question: "But how happens it that he who is said to enjoy these things is so commonly a *poor* civilized man, while the savage, who has them not, is rich as a savage?" Of course, Thoreau makes these points, in part, to justify his own experiment in simplified living. It's not lost on me that a bachelor with no children could find a tool shed, boxcar, or 150 square foot cabin sufficient for all his needs.

The second time we visited Walden Pond, I was forty-four, Thoreau's age when he died. I'd been married twenty years and had three young children in tow. The main purpose of the trip was so our children could experience the history of downtown Boston, and I was worried we might not make it to Concord and Lexington. Fortunately, New England was experiencing a heatwave, and after a day walking the Freedom Trail in a hundred degree weather, discovering that few businesses had air conditioning, and realizing that when it was this hot in Texas, we seldom venture outdoors, we decided to take the kids swimming. And where better to swim than Walden Pond?

"I feel like they've finally been baptized," I said, sitting on the shore with Christa watching our children splash, laughing, happy for the break from their father's running commentary on why *every single* place we'd visited was significant, important, and interesting.

"They were all baptized when they were born," she said. "You were there."

"I know," I said, "but now they've swam in the same water as Thoreau."

"And now probably peed where he peed."

"Still," I said. "It makes me happy."

"I'm glad," she said.

At some point in the day, we stopped by the Shop at Walden Pond where I convinced myself again that the cabin blueprints were overpriced, extraneous to the simple life. Instead, I discovered back issues of *The Concord Saunterer*, and bought one to read while the children swam. Sitting on the water's edge, I started thinking about the things I knew, intellectually, about Thoreau, about this place, this water. I was transported back to the suburbs of Ft. Worth, back to my days as a high school senior, trying to envision the exact spot I was seated. When the blue and green waters of Walden Pond had seemed as distant and magical to me as the moon.

"What're you looking at?" Christa asked, taking a break from her book.

"I'm trying to see if the water changes color," I said.

"I think all water does, depending on the time of day."

Not like this water, I thought but didn't say it aloud. While Christa does not share my obsession with Thoreau, she tolerates it, encourages it, listens to me talk about it. She probably knew the gist of what I was thinking, and since we were *literally* sitting on the shore of Walden Pond, quoting something from Thoreau would have added nothing to the moment. It was enough to be there, to be awake, to focus on seeing what I was seeing. Which was our children lost in the pure joy of water.

The next day we knocked around Concord, and found our way to Sleepy Hollow Cemetery, the final resting place of Thoreau, Ralph Waldo Emerson, Nathaniel Hawthorne, and Louisa May Alcott. Christa and I had visited the cemetery on our honeymoon, remembered its rolling hills, soft grass, evergreens and oaks. The perfect spot for a picnic. We located Thoreau's grave that is marked with a book-sized stone that simply reads *Henry*, adorned with a ring of acorns, so unlike Emerson's massive rose quartz marker and bronze plaque. Everyone's favorite that day, however, was Louisa May Alcott's grave because school children had written notes they tucked beneath rocks on her grave telling her how much they loved reading *Little Women*.

A picture from that afternoon sits on my cluttered desk. Christa is seated on the ground with our three children hunched in a semicircle around her, watching her prepare sandwiches. The children are partially shaded with ribbons of sunlight covering their blond hair and baby faces. Each time I look at it, I'm transported once again, feeling melancholy that they are now teenagers, making plans to find a world of their own, but also joyful for these moments of the sublime. My hope is that someday if asked what their parents were like, my children will say: *the type of people who liked to picnic in cemeteries.*

Many parts of *Walden* find Thoreau waxing nostalgic, which is understandable given that, in the seven years he spent revising the text, he's always looking backwards to a time he spent two years living in semi-solitude, grieving the death of his beloved brother. At times, however, his reveries become problematic as in "Former Inhabitants; and Winter Visitors" when he mentions the Black men and women, some formerly enslaved, who once lived in the Walden woods. Thoreau calls them "dusky," suggests the land they attempted to scratch a living from is sterile, and concludes, "how little does the memory of these human inhabitants enhance the beauty of the landscape!" Thoreau offers no reason as to why Black residents of the Concord area might have been relegated to spaces where it was difficult to make a living. Neither does he seem to wonder where their descendants might be living in the present. Rather, he ends the section thus: "With such reminiscences I repeopled the woods and lulled myself to sleep." By "repeopling," of course, Thoreau means that he engaged in an imaginative exercise, bringing the Black men and women back to the woods for an afternoon. However, it's difficult to overcome the reality that beautiful landscapes and manicured towns like Concord were (and so often are) primarily, if not exclusively, white spaces.

Those familiar with Thoreau's "Slavery in Massachusetts" or his multiple essays extolling the American abolitionist, John Brown, or even the night Thoreau spent in prison for tax evasion, refusing to support a government that supported slavery, and especially the work Thoreau and his family did with the Underground Railroad, might bristle at my suggestion that Thoreau didn't do enough to advance the cause of Black people in America. And that's fair. It's difficult not to notice, however, that whether he's imaging the Black people who once lived in Walden Woods or providing a fugitive enslaved person with a place to stay for the night pointing him "forward toward the north star," he always seems to be ushering Black bodies from one place to another.

The past few years I've reflected more on who "peoples" the spaces I inhabit, the neighborhoods in which I've lived, the churches and schools I've attended, the clubs and organizations who have welcomed me in, and I realize they are primarily white spaces, not by accident, but by design. And so, if I read Thoreau with a critical eye, I have to read my own narratives the same way. For most of my life, I've asked, "who else should be at the table?" and "what voices can I amplify?" Now I'm asking, "where should I step aside?" and "who should I be listening to?"

On my forty-fifth birthday, when I ripped wrapping paper from a cardboard cylinder, I was at a loss. I had long since passed the age of hanging posters of sports figures or musicians on my wall. A certificate declaring *A Star Has Been Named in Your Honor!* seemed unlikely.

"Just open it," Christa said.

"Well, let me think," I said.

The children groaned. An annoying ritual in our family involves the gift-recipient attempting to guess the contents before opening. In fairness, it's more of a "me" ritual, performed mainly for my amusement, but once a character has been developed, I feel it's important to play the part.

"It's from the online Shop at Walden Pond," Christa said.

"It's not," I said.

"It is," she said.

I carefully sliced the packing tape, popped out the plastic end stop, and removed seven thin sheets of paper—blueprints of Thoreau's cabin.

"I always thought the price tag was outrageous," I said.

"I know," Christa said.

"I love it."

"I know."

Christa is a consumption enabler. I covet objects and experiences, all while delivering my stock phrases: *beautiful but not worth it; nice if you've got the money; where in the world would we put it?* I always want to save for retirement, save for the children's education, save for land in the country, save for a rainy day. I'm always afraid we'll have to ask our parents for money (which we have), that we'll go broke (which we've done), that we'll have to work until we die (which remains to be to be seen). I desperately want to play the role of the cheapskate, the skinflint, the faithful child of people who were raised by people who survived the Great Depression.

However, I love stuff I don't need. Like blueprints for a cabin I'll never build, like a ceramic Thoreau figurine, like seven different editions of *Walden,* like a Walden shower curtain for my bathroom.

And shoes. God almighty I love a nice pair of shoes.

A list of my current inventory for dress shoes: one pair of light purple suede; one pair of faded red suede; one navy cloth; black and gray faux alligator; two-tone light and dark blue wingtips; two-tone maroon and black leather; two identical pairs that differ in that one pair is gray with blue shoe laces, the other, brown with red shoe laces; light brown wingtips; suede with green soles; black with blue tartan, purchased on the Edinburgh Royal Mile; tricolor leather from a shop in Bath; a pair of faux leather shoes that contain all three primary and all three secondary colors; and one necessary pair of solid black dress shoes. I also have two pairs of cowboy boots, and six pairs of Converse tennis shoes.

Some people have more shoes. Some have less. I always want more.

In *Walden,* Thoreau identified clothing as one of the four essentials for living. About footwear, he contends: "bare feet are older than shoes, and he can make them do." The thing is, when I am at home, I always prefer bare feet. I wear shoes while cutting grass and running a weed eater, but that's about it. I'll use a chainsaw, jigsaw, circular saw, and chop saw in bare feet. I remodeled our kitchen, which involved sledgehammers to remove pantry and closet walls, hanging sheetrock, replacing parts of the ceiling, dismantling fifty-year-old cabinets and constructing new ones, relocating appliances, and rerouting electrical outlets. And, I did it all in bare feet. If it were socially acceptable to attend church, social events, and work functions *sans* footwear, I might never wear shoes.

I *want* to simplify my life, to live simply, to simplify, simplify, simplify, to eat the green beans whose rows I hoe, barefooted, but the problem is I also want to drink expensive Scotch while wearing handcrafted, red leather shoes.

I repeatedly fail the limestone test, collecting things that require dusting but never enough, apparently, to fill me with disgust or terror. The irony is that even though I derive great joy from consumption, I have never wanted to work for a living, something that should nudge me closer to a life of simplification. The echoes of my dilemma are found, of course, in

Walden, especially the parts in which he (problematically) recounts his interactions with, and opinions of, Irish immigrants.

What's commonly known as the Irish Potato Famine occurred between the years 1845 and 1849 when a blight struck one of the main food sources for the Irish, causing mass hunger and starvation, and a wave of Irish emigration to the shores of the United States. Many of these Irish immigrants found work constructing the railroad that cut across the edge of Walden woods. Thoreau has much to say about this railroad and the Irish who helped build it.

In "Economy," he imagines "a million Irishmen starting up from all the shanties in the land" asking "is not this railroad which we have built a good thing?" To which Thoreau answers, "Yes . . . *comparatively* good, that is, you might have done worse; but I wish, as you are brothers of mine, that you could have spent your time better than digging in this dirt." This seems a harsh response to people laboring in a new country at tasks that have historically been relegated, in large part, *only* to people who are new to the United States.

Later in "Where I Lived, and What I Lived For," Thoreau attempts to create a kinship with these recent immigrants when he writes:

We do not ride on the railroad; it rides upon us. Did you ever think what those sleepers are that underlie the railroad? Each one is a man, an Irishman, or a Yankee man. The rails are laid on them, and they are covered with sand, and the cars run smoothly over them. They are sound sleepers, I assure you. And every few years a new lot is laid down and run over; so that, if some have the pleasure of riding on a rail, others have the misfortune to be ridden upon.... Why should we live with such hurry and waste of life?

Thoreau critiques what we might, in the twenty-first century, call global capitalism. He highlights how our need for convenience and speed often comes at a human and environmental cost that we often don't see. We can metaphorically ride upon the rails without giving much thought to the lives of those laying the rails, the invisible labor, those who are being ground into dust.

I could, if I chose, be reminded of this often when my writing is interrupted by our dogs barking because a driver is delivering a book to my front porch. A book I decided only recently that I needed. From the dusty shelves of a bookstore yesterday to the dusty stacks that crowd my desk today.

Thoreau spills the most ink on an Irishman named John Fields, "an honest, hard-working, but shiftless man," married with many children. Thoreau tried to convince Fields that he wouldn't need to work so hard at menial labor if only Fields would simplify his life. Too many people come to America, Thoreau argues, for the pleasures of having "tea and coffee and meat everyday." The pursuit of such commodities are what drive us into the dust. "If he and his family would live simply," Thoreau contends, "they might all go a-huckleberrying in the summer for their amusement."

John Fields "heaved a sigh at this," and anyone with a partner and/or children of their own, and bills to pay, might sigh right along with honest John.

Don't get me wrong: the sighing, doesn't change the fact that neither John, nor Henry David, nor I necessarily *want* to work for a living. To say aloud, however, "I don't want to work" is problematic for many people, for many reasons. It smacks of privilege and entitlement to those *unable* to work or those who find themselves underemployed, to those who work two or three jobs to pay for rent, groceries, and medicine for their families. Not working is also an unthinkable option at this point in my life, what with a mortgage, two car payments, three teenagers, and an affinity for Scotch and nice shoes.

Nonetheless, I *really* hate to work.

Allow me to clarify one point: by "work," I mean the kind you do in exchange for money. I love to be occupied; I'll spend ten uninterrupted hours in the lawn, painting or building something or days on end researching and writing.

The main reason I dislike work for hire is a thing I'm even more hesitant to admit than the fact that I don't want to work at all, something that I had not realized until I reflected on the *why:* the tasks I enjoy most are done in solitude. And if I know one thing about the court of public opinion, it's this: people are suspicious of someone who wants to be alone. In a cabin. In the woods.

A few years ago, I built a greenhouse in my backyard. To construct this twenty-four square foot structure, I used instructions from a DIY manual as a starting point. Innovation and necessity took over the project as I sketched modifications and pivoted on the fly. The greenhouse came in over budget and over time, but I take great pride in the finished product. And, it's still standing.

A few months after I completed the greenhouse, my teenage son and I were playing *Monopoly* in my home office.

"Are those the plans you used to make the greenhouse?" my son asked.

At first, I was confused by his question. A stack of DIY books were perched on the side on my enormous writing desk, but they were closed, half-buried in layers of paperwork.

"What?" I asked. "No. What are you talking about?"

He pointed to where one sheet of the Walden cabin blueprints is mounted on a sliver of wall between two windows.

"Sh-eesh. No," I said. "I can't believe I didn't even think about that."

"Epic fail, dad," he said.

And indeed, it felt like an epic fail.

"You owe me fourteen hundred dollars," he said.

"For what?"

"Park Place. Three houses. Fourteen hundred bucks," he said.

"I don't have fourteen-hundred bucks," I said.

"Yeah, me neither, but I'm about to," he said. "Start mortgaging property."

So much of what Thoreau writes about in *Walden* is about being awake, about seeing what others miss, about paying close attention to the world around us. How had I squandered the opportunity to build a Thoreau-cabin, replica greenhouse? Me, of all people. I have the blueprints. I have daydreamed about that cabin, about what it represents, since I was eighteen years old.

I am not alone, of course, in this desire to create a physical and/or mental, Thoreau-inspired space. Dozens of books and articles have been written about people's efforts to recreate Thoreau's cabin. You can take a college class and build a close approximation. And, there is no shortage of videos, television shows, and how-to books dedicated to the tiny house movement. My own plans to build a cabin stemmed from a desire to create a quiet space where I could read and write. Even though our house is sprawling with many rooms, for years, it was cluttered with furniture, toys, school projects, litter boxes—all the necessary debris of two adults and three young children. And nary a corner in which one could sit to hear themselves think.

"I'd like to build a writing shed in the backyard," I would say often.

"You could," Christa would say.

"The problem," I would say, "is that I can't write in the dark, but most times of the year, it'll be too hot."

"Well, we'd run electricity to it," she would say.

"Would we?"

"Why wouldn't we?"

"It's the spirit of the thing I worry about."

"Oh that," she would say.

And so, the cabin could never come to fruition in a way that I wanted it to function, literally or symbolically.

For her sixteenth birthday, our oldest daughter wanted to take a trip back to Boston, which meant, of course, that I lobbied for a day trip to Walden Pond. I had forgotten to bring a hat on this trip and have reached the age where a sunburnt bald head concerns me, and so we stopped by the Shop at Walden and the amazing new welcome center. Truth be told, the main reason I wanted to visit the gift shop was to browse back issues of *The Concord Saunterer*. And not just any random issue, but a specific one that contains an article about the waterlily Thoreau uses as a metaphor at the end of "Slavery in Massachusetts." To my delight, the volume in question was on the shelf.

"See, here's the article I wrote," I said to my daughter, holding open the journal. "That's neat, dad," she said. "Good job."

Even though I have several copies of the journal at home and surely, I'd shown it to my children when it had come out years before, my teenage self was excited seeing it in the Shop at Walden itself. In my own small way, I had become the type of person who tries to explain what Thoreau was thinking about when he was thinking about nature. And so, I doffed my new Walden Pond baseball cap, satisfied to be on vacation, and joined my wife and daughter to spend the afternoon swimming in a pond the size of a lake.

Thoreau apologists often argue that Thoreau's work does more good than harm: *Walden* almost single-handedly spurred the American environmentalist movement. In my thirty-five-year journey with the text, I've made similar arguments along the way. However, I don't think we can absolve or ignore Thoreau's somewhat misguided views on race and immigrants simply because he was a product of his time. At the same time, it's fair to ask: can one be wrongheaded about some things, *and* lead a righteous movement? Perhaps. Regardless, I don't think we should discard Thoreau and his text because he is problematic in many areas any more than we should diminish his offensive views in order to highlight only passages of beautiful American nature writing. Thoreau, like his beloved pond, (like his readers, perhaps) is, after all "blue at one time and green at another, even from the same point of view." Grappling with the tension and contradictions within the text of *Walden* is at the heart of why Thoreau moved to the woods for two years and then spent the next seven years writing about it, which was an attempt, in part, to answer a very good question: what does it mean to be a broken human being living in a broken world?

Burnt Bones of Our Home

Dave Malone

Most summers, I drive ten hours
back to the burnt bones of our home.
To that little hill that shrinks
year by year. To that little lake

that nudges closer and closer
to the back yard where I crafted
a five-hole golf course
that twisted around cedar and pine,

Play-Doh cannisters as cups
for birdies and bogies
against stiff Kansas winds.
Below the greens stirred

the old creek bed
where the First Americans
made fire, hauled water
from the spring-fed lake,

told stories, became ghosts,
before I was. And here I am
solstice after solstice
on this fading knoll

where the pine are gone,
the prairie grasses
long dead, the cedar berries
crushed and deceased,

where nothing great
lives here anymore,
not the Kanza, not
my hard-working father.

Foxtails

Donna D. Vitucci

Empty Nest

Caryn Mirriam-Goldberg

> "The house was quiet and the world was calm."
> ~ Wallace Stevens

The house is empty and the world isn't calm.
The dog is quiet and the porch is dappled
with power tools, screws losing their grip,
and a hammock swaying in the dusty arms
of the sky, which tips everything out of it.

The inside is outside, and the universe is all
the rooms at once, this bright varying light
called blue, then orange or gray, raining
or inhaling to make something else out of itself.

The traveling is inherent, and the child is gone.
Home is a placeholder and time a room rearranged,
its inhabitants shifted and necessities eased.
The floors are wide and the doorknobs lonely.

The house is full and the world?
The world is listening for what comes next.

A Kansas Photographer's Inspiration

Karen Colstrom

As a Kansas photographer, my inspiration is of prairie, pastureland, wildflowers, sunrises and sunsets. So many things to be inspired by in the country. After my husband and I moved to the family farm and built a small house, I started photographing the countryside. I discovered so much beauty in the landscape. My husband and I talk about how peaceful and amazing it is to be out on the farm. In the evening, we go out walking and enjoy nature, the sky, the stars, and the moon.

Why are we driven to capture nature's beauty? Perhaps some people may not see it at all....one needs to experience it. My love of photography became more than just a hobby. It became a passion. I want to share what I find. A photographer finds the beauty that surrounds us and captures the fleeting moment.

In an instant you can capture a sunrise or sunset. There is an emotion. Each photo tells a story. That story may be of a season, the weather, a butterfly, or a simple flower.

As a photographer, I display and sell my photographs. I share my story. People will come talk to me at art shows and share their stories as well. I have met so many wonderful people that love the Kansas countryside. We talk about the old farmsteads, windmills, butterflies, the experiences of a sunrise or a sunset. People share what they have seen. It is a compliment to me that people stop and take the time to reminisce about their life and what they have experienced.

A photograph can bring back happy memories of home, or growing up as a child, a memory of what once was.... A part of our history of a long time ago.

This is my inspiration as a photographer of country landscapes and prairie.

Capturing Kansas' beauty.

A place that I call home.

Apricots

Caryn Mirriam-Goldberg

Hold an apricot in your palm,
no bouncy ball, miniature planet,
water balloon, robin's egg,
just a velvet skinned orb
of sour, sweet, the definition
of a wry smile from someone
you've known a long time
or just caught the eye of
from across the street.

Between its flesh and pit,
a shimmy of space,
then the taste you think
will save you at this moment
like day lilies save a ruined garden
of a bad day right before
the sun oranges everything
into darkness.

Asemic Text w285

Gregory Stump

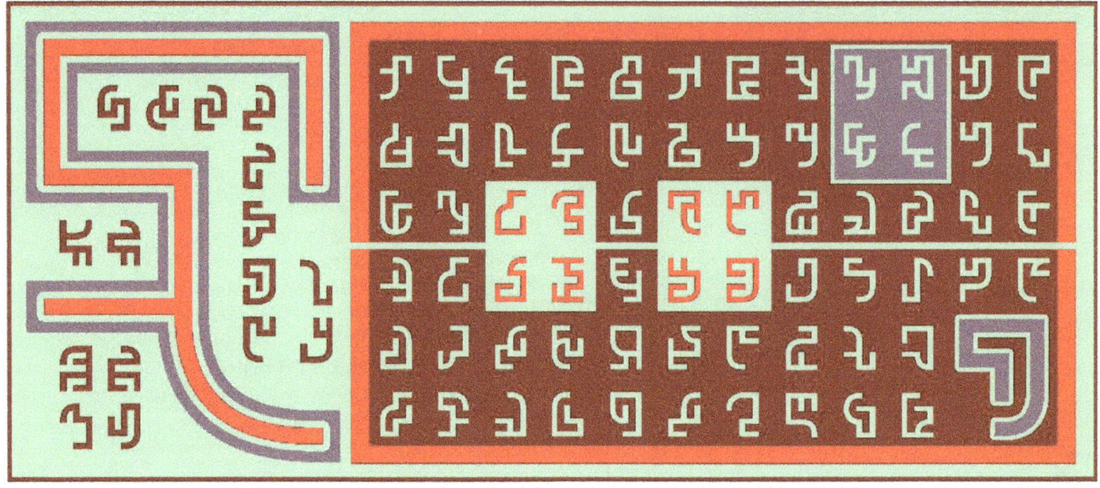

Covid When Daylight Savings Time Kicks In

Caryn Mirriam-Goldberg

Stop, you benign bonus light. I'm begging
thermometers and damp skies for mercy.
Too cold, too hot in the empty vault
of what I thought was my life but is just
so much office furniture and clanging lamps.

Day, you promised rain but don't deliver
so I'm back in bed with the ceiling and the cat,
the mottled wind banging its knuckles
on the window, waking me again.

Winter flocks, where have you gone?
I've even put out sunflower seed you love,
now gone to wind, squirrels, and all those
plugging their tasksinto bright slots of doings
despite time not being what it ws 24 hours ago.

Oh bed and couch, I can only subtract naps
from the hum and surges of the washing machine,
another Covid test with two lines, and so much green
scribbling its presence across flowers, wasps, rabbits.

Sky, you don't belong to anyone, but please
breathe me back into time.

A View of the Interstate

Enda M. Brennan

My landlord's landscapers weed-whacked my wildflower garden last weekend. The flowers weren't meticulously planted; just a sowing mix. I'd spent a day crouched in the abandoned bed by my back stairs tilling the hard soil with a trowel. Another day spent raking the surface and spreading handfuls of seeds before sprinkling a shallow layer of potting mix on top. I'd never grown flowers from seed before and it was magical watching them sprout. Each morning, I would dash out to check on them while my coffee percolated, swelling with pride at their haphazard progress and excited to see what sort of flowers ended up where.

When I came home from work and stepped out to water them in the dim light from my neighbor's porch, I blinked, confused, at their absence. I stared at the grass cuttings that lay about the lawn, branches strewn messily to the perimeters, and realized in an instant the culling that had occurred.

I spent a good while crouched by the empty bed, looking at the severed stalks and crushed leaves, pressing my fingers against the cool, soft ground while tears flowed freely. I felt wounded, and childishly so. My cheeks stung. I felt angry at the landscapers but more so furious with myself because I wasn't there to advocate for the fledgling plants, to let people know they aren't just weeds -- those are flowers. They're still growing. Even though they were in a brick-edged bed I should have put up a sign. I should have known better that most people would see only disarray in an unkept space whereas I saw potential to bloom.

I love wildflowers. These cheery souls that seem to live aloft on the wind and brighten unexpected corners. Just as I love birds and bugs and all the other beings that people largely take for granted. Maybe I love the neglected things because I still don't know how to love myself. Regardless, I should have been there to speak for the defenseless flowers I was cultivating, at least partially reliant on me for protection and sustenance. Just as I would want someone to speak for me.

I hate that many wildflowers are determined arbitrarily to be "weeds" by humans who see indigenous nature as an interruption on their own, superimposed design. When, in reality, these mix of "weeds" and their hardy roots would have done the effort of softening the soil in these fallow beds, making them more arable for future, more "sophisticated" plantings.

It is devastating to think of dandelions, clovers, etc uprooted out of manicured lawns; burned and tossed away so they can't take root again. I've so often been cast out of places just because I don't fit the bigger picture. Told to get out, stay away. Don't come back. Years and years and a hundred different places and a thousand rejections and interventions and cast arrows of disapproval, half a dozen zipcodes in quick succession, all the towns I've felt chased out of if not by torch or pitchfork than simply by worn-out welcome. All that and then some – countless professions of affections – but still no one has ever once asked me to stay.

Go away. We are better off without you.

Once my ex boyfriend told me that no one should plant flowers in a garden because they don't have a purpose. I puzzled over this for days, weeks. How can a flower not have a purpose? They are beautiful and they feed bees. They make people smile. No, they don't have much to exploit for human consumption, but they are far from useless.

It occurred to me later that he could never love me.

I remember when I was a kid we built this fort into the crevices between two giant boulders that were half-embedded into a hill that lay about a quarter mile into the woods that sat across from our house. It's hard to describe. But you'd walk up this trail going towards the meadow and the horse fields beyond. The trail rose gradually then dropped off suddenly as you realized the slight incline was caused by landfill around these big granite slabs. The kind you see all over in New England, the ones that are just as big as our snow drifts, great rocks that beckon to be scaled.

We built a whole little world into the tiny "caves" created by the odd intersections of these boulders. One part was jagged like steps, so that became steps to a lookout. There were places to hide on your belly, to sit and talk knee to knee, we had a "kitchen" where we stashed all the shards of pottery we'd chance upon in the marshes on our archeological digs; rocks that could be arrowheads. We brought tarps to lash between trees to create sunrooms. Looking back it probably looked like an adult someone was camping out in the woods, but it was our place. The best Fort that ever was or would be.

All the neighborhood kids would rest and regroup and conspire at the Fort between our treks through the woodland marshes that lay between the interstate highway and our neighborhood. Our games of "Indian" and "Indian" (none of us cared much for cowboys.) Of "olden days"; games of soldier and paleontologist. Sometimes I'd pretend to be someone from mythology -- Odysseus bushwacking his way across a hostile island, Atalanta outrunning every man who challenged her up so many rocky slopes. I'd try to walk without making a single noise like I heard the Wampanoag could do because they knew the land and paid attention.

All the meticulously planned excursions, the secrets, the important things that all children do in the forest when adults aren't around to be nosy.

Because everything was so important then, wasn't it? When we were children? Grave Endeavors. The weight of possibility, a new chapter of a serial adventure spanning each day between the finishing of homework and streetlight call to dinner.

They started building a subdivision near the entrance to that section of the woods. I think it was the year I turned eleven. The year before they found the malignant basal cells three inches from my optic nerve. The same year my friend's mother died of glioblastoma, the third of my parents' friends in just a few years. It was three years after they closed our town dump, the one that was on the Superfund list, the one where they found all the enriched uranium. It was five years before I started doing drugs, before I started nosing around in the abandoned jewelry factories that littered our industrial landscape, thinking all the time about my mother's warning of unstable floors in those buildings but never once about the asbestos or potassium cyanide.

The construction gradually encroached more and more up the trail as spring progressed into long-shadowed summer. Then one day, nailed to a tree nearby the section of the trail just before the rock formation became apparent, was a warning of a future blasting. They were going to blow up our rocks. It said the date and time. Warned us to keep away.

We were distraught. Myself and my two closest playmates ran to rally the troops. We all put our heads together and decided to write a manifesto. We nailed it to the tree on top of the blast notice. I brought the hammer and nails.

It said Attention: this is Our Rock.

It said that we had found it. That it might look like any other rock, but it wasn't -- it was Ours and it was important and special and it was our fort and nevermind why we need it -- we just do and you can't have it. It implored them to please blow up a different rock. Please build this subdivision somewhere else. This was ours.

And of course, like all children who find themselves righteously rallied against some aspect of the adult world, we actually thought that would work. We thought the demolition crew would find our letter and be moved to call off the blast.

That innocent, burning earnestness.

I don't think I ever grew out of that.

Of course it didn't work. They blew up our rock. I remember going the day after the blast was scheduled and seeing the tree we had tagged with our Treatise clinging to the side of a giant crater. The rocks were whiter on the inside than the outside and covered all in a fine red dust. Little pulverized pieces of stone and dirt and tree roots lining the bottom of the crater. Wires from the blasting.

We amused ourselves for a while using exposed tree roots to scale one side of the crater, but a game of mountaineer can only be stretched so far. We milled around, finding shreds of tarp. A piece of a toy we had found and stashed earlier in the summer. Shards of pottery pulverized further. We tried to rebuild the fort at another site, but it just wasn't the same, and we were all starting to grow out of the use for forts, as you do. Or so you are led to believe.

The destruction of this fort was the beginning of the end. It was the start of about five years of developing the woods across from my house into back-to-back cul-du-sacs. Day by day, from the ages of eleven until around sixteen, I watched the woods where we played disappear. The fort was just the surface. There were so many things throughout those woods, all the important places plotted onto maps we labored over in basements on rainy days. The marsh-head plants that looked like wigwams. The mossy stones. The creek. The stoney bridge. The top five trees for climbing. The "quarry" which was really just a hole full of flagstones. Three places where you might be able to find geodes. The fastest route to pet the horses.

Gone now. All of it. And I watched them take it away. The noise of it. The violence. The backhoes and bulldozers.

The worst part was the way that the concrete foundations sat empty for years. It took them so long to build the houses after clearing our woods. I don't remember how long, but at least two winters. Because we played hockey in the basements. They'd fill up with water and freeze over in the winter, creating a skating rink. Which was fun. But I still wished we could have had the woods for a few more years.

Seven years later my parents left the state altogether, citing a desire to live into their 60s. This severed my ties with those woods, that swamp, those friends – many of whom weren't lucky enough to leave that town before heroin caught up with them in a region where a narcotic prescription for a torn ACL junior year might as well be a death sentence. Summer before college I found myself, for better or worse, uprooted.

These days I drift and drift and alight for a season. I still struggle to trust the soil. I've tried to get better about it, try to let people in, let them know me. These little exercises in investment, in permanence. Like planting a flower garden, only to have my hopes, as usual, dashed upon the ground. Lately it feels like I am scrambling to hold onto a wet rock on shore. The memories of a childhood spent studying moss and befriending bugs and garter snakes, of exploring the entire universe contained in a tide pool down Narragansett – these thoughts make me ache, ache with knowledge of a world that no longer exists. The memories of how, over the course of my childhood, I watched so much of the land I loved in my region disappear. And how no one could really explain to me why this was acceptable.

Sometimes I feel silly. For still crying full-force over things like a weed-whacked flower bed and for the loss of the woods I loved twenty-five years after the fact.

But these days I'm more determined than ever to continue to be the sort of person who would cry over a trampled flower, who would sit with a dying bird, help a toad off the sidewalk. Even if it feels silly.

It's not silly.

It never is.

A ~~Poet~~ (Mom) Delivers Her Own Eulogy

Victoria James

I ask that you don't cry for me, don't drench your heart
with sorrow. If you could tap into my most sacred
memories, you would only smile.

Open up my mind to see Polaroids captured for safe keeping.
Find the joy there, see it filter life through my every vein.

I lived it and thank God I did.

I heard the warm soft "dada" every morning.
The flap of his little hand like bird wings, saying hello.
I watched dad light up anytime his son looked in his direction.

Aching knees bent low just to read a bedtime story —
interrupted by erupting "dada" and more bird wings.

Thump, thump, thump, thump
across the old hardwood floors of his sprinting crawls.

I witnessed dad hold an inconsolable baby
like it was his greatest treasure,
the world was pure in those moments.

I was part of creating core memories for my husband
and son — unforgettable joy we'd relive *(even in death)*.

Don't cry for me because how lucky *(God how lucky)*
was I to be given *any* time with my little family.

Let them come to you. Let them talk your ear off
about those memories. Listen to them choose you,
say your name. Let them wave at you like bird wings.

Because that's all I ever needed.

Asemic Text w338

Gregory Stump

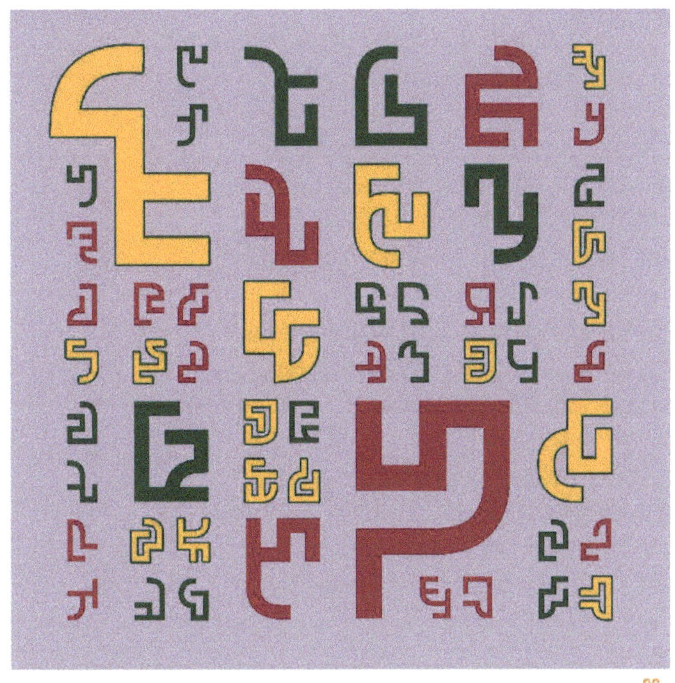

Motherhood on 11x17 Canvas, Mixed Media

Victoria James

I'm a cool palate, blue, purple, green -
I wish - reality, I'm warm: spicy red, sour yellow, sticky orange -
the colors of candy nobody likes.

Throw me on a Canvas every which way:
Palette knife me down, smear my edges to keep
me in place. Water me down to spread me thinner
to use me more than I'm meant for.

Blood red blends with velvet cream.
Bag up the .5oz of strawberry milk glaze,
throw it, sculpt it, burn it in the kiln.
Title the sculpture, Failed Attempt at Breastfeeding.

Mix me with alcohol ink and watch me
swing hazy, dance lazy, and think crazy
all over the paper, forgetting every direction.

Step back, look at the masterpiece:
She's a little dysfunctional, a little messy,
a mixed media piece of sorts, but damn
what a picture she's made. An artist.

The Supermodels

Jenn Dean

Mid-summer mornings feel heavy, as if the color green has weight. Maples with branches lathered with moss and leaves big as platters overhang the roads. Even the air feels overripe and pliant. Up on the escarpment, the luminous milky plume of Snoqualmie Falls thunders over Tertiary basalt and tuff: an exhalation of rock and air and water. From the road I feel the river pouring over the cliff's granite belly like a liquid thundercloud.

On the upper plateau I drive past ancient rail cars rusted in place like fossilized sections of a Jurassic python in old town Snoqualmie, then whiz across the prairie, zig-zag through North Bend, and arrive a few minutes later at a dead end: the Olallie State Forest, thirty-eight miles east of Seattle. A trail follows the south fork of the Snoqualmie, and winds through the dense jungled understory. The water shines green and gold. Immense sun-dappled boulders lounge in the middle of the flow like elephants and fly fishermen angle into shallow pools. The sun casts crystals across the wide braided reach, and salmonberry and lacelike vine maple hang thick on the banks. Devils club dangles leaves as big as islands above my head.

The trail winds a mile to the top, where a vertigo-inspiring footbridge spans a two-tiered fall. But it's the woods I've come to see. Uprooted from my native oaks, beeches, and mixed hardwoods of New England, since landing here I've gradually absorbed the flora and fauna, in search of what one novelist calls the 'poetry of survival,' a poetry that feels harder to grasp now that I'm in my sixties. For people even older than myself, the concept of aging-in-place was born, so elders can avoid the indignities of a nursing home. Whether I am bathed or clothed, or worse, drooling, the woods feel like a release from the Psychocene, an era when we attach ourselves to little rectangles in order to witness our own destruction. Today, I'm looking for the ultimate aging-in-placers.

I follow the trail up a steep rise to a bench, where I take in the view from afar. Framed by thick forests, a waterfall sluices down through the evergreens: liquid glass over a two-hundred-foot shale cliff. Below, the river meanders in and out of view, dotted with boulders. Light cascades through the canopy, and plashes of sun light up the chive-green leaves.

A few traverses of the rocky dirt path later, a tree—though that word doesn't aptly describe it—sits down an incline from the path, along a spur that leads to the cobbled shore of the river. If you were hell bent on getting to the falls, you'd miss it, for it grows far enough off the path to obscure its base, big and round as a grain silo. A *Pseudotsuga menziesii,* or Douglas fir. I approach slowly, as one would do an animal, and stare upwards. The bole dives up into the sky. Short branches start fifty feet up, all reaching to one side; on the other side several withered limbs stick out. It appears the crown had been struck by lightning or fell off. If one carved out the base, it would make a suitable four-story dwelling.

Her crenellated bark holds long deep furrows, each giant flake replete with little holes and smaller flakes. Along the bark weave paths of slug slime, and among the crevasses spiders stretch small webs, the bark an apartment complex for who knows how many myriad insects. Beetles heave around the base like guards and ants cross the tree's roots near the bottom as if circumnavigating a mountain; a worn path circles her bole. I place both hands on her skin, then walk slowly around her. On the opposite side, the tree supports a young western hemlock, whose roots start far above my head and look like octopus limbs as they pipe down to the ground. Licorice ferns stick out like green hands, and the bark resembles abraded skin.

I withdraw a long nylon rope from my backpack and let the end rest on the bark at about chest height from the ground, circle the trunk again, then tie the string off and mark it. It measures eighteen feet in circumference, or (divided by π) just under 6 feet in diameter. I multiply the diameter in inches by the growth factor for Douglas fir (5, which means it takes 5 years to put on an inch of girth) which reveals the tree's approximate age: three hundred and sixty years, which makes it older than our unraveling democracy. Taking the Little Ice Age into account, which slowed growth for over three hundred years, I arbitrarily add 140 years to the tree's life, and give it a birthdate of 1520.

I sit with my back up against the bark and open a thermos of caffeine. Not many are aware of this, but one of the largest mining operations in the Pacific Northwest operates in this forest right underneath my derriere. Thousands of workers have painstakingly bored tunnels into the feldspar and hornblende and other rocks in all directions as they search for magnesium, iron, and other minerals. The miners, mischievous daredevils who like to serve up the occasional semi-poisonous meal, don't wear headlamps, or protective gear. They are fungi, uniquely suited to underground conditions. Their fungal threads, or hyphae, extend for miles. Thinner than tapeworms, the hyphae, which merge with the root-hair tips of trees and plants, serve up a slurry of nitrogen, phosphorous, calcium, and potassium. In return, the fungal threads receive a cocktail of carbon and sugar from the tree's root tips. Scientists call this mutualism; non-scientists like myself call it sharing.

The trees work the connections on the fungal map, or mycorrhizal network, like frenzied 1950's stockbrokers on landlines, sending carbon or messages of insect infestations, which signal other trees to turn on their defensive enzymes. Dump carbon! Release the phenolic heteropolymers! A forest is anything but static. If insects or animals get around the structural leaf defenses of wax, thorn, or a leather-like coating, a simple needle chomp by an invader elicits a chemical slurry.

Logging companies, who clear native plants and 'weed trees' like birch, and burn slash, rip the digestive system right out of the forest. They plant seedlings of all the same species, who have no historical networks of mycorrhizas to nourish and protect them. And no mother trees, which have been found to nourish whole colonies of their offspring. Forests empty of old trees, and thus mycorrhizas, are more prone to disease, less healthy, less "productive" as future timber. That we know this is predominantly due to Susan Simard, a sixty-something-year-old British Columbian forester, researcher, and professor, who, like most women in male-dominated arenas, was scoffed at by her male peers and the scientific community throughout the nascent stages of her research, and ridiculed as her published studies, all of which held up to peer review and replication, came to the fore. Her work promulgated the term the "Wood Wide Web," when the gold-standard journal *Nature* published her dissertation findings.[1]

Simard suggests that like humans, trees seek connection, diversity, and community. Here the nomenclature gets persnickety—science likes more objective words like "need" over "seek," "mutualism" rather than "share." The big tree at my back—what Simard calls a Mother Tree, old trees with myriad relationships developed over time, trees that feed and nurture the forest as a whole--infuses a body with memory, as if memory were as solid as air, solid as rock. It has a fixity that I envy. And it very much feels like a *who*, not an "it."

If George Vancouver charted the Northwest coast today, he'd find a vastly different landscape than the one he sailed into during his 1791-1795 expedition. When he left the open ocean and coasted into the estuary—the second largest in the country at 95 miles long and five miles wide in some places—he saw, where Seattle's port is today, food-rich tidelands that fanned out from the lower Duwamish (one of many rivers that emptied into the sound). The sound consisted of a huge tidal gash left by the retreat of the ice sheet, pocked with weirdly shaped islands: a tide-filled saltwater wound. On modern maps it appears as if a swimming giant stuck their hand into the land from the Pacific, bent their wrist southward, wiggled their fingers around, then withdrew; the resulting watery shape hooks around the coastal Olympic range, then dives south almost a hundred miles. The largest cities west of the Cascades—Tacoma, Seattle—lie sandwiched between the coast range to the west and the Cascades to the east, and sit starboard on the large multi-fingered waterway we now call the Salish Sea. Pocked with islands, bays, marshes, and underwater canyons, and ringed by volcanoes, the waterway's northern lid—Vancouver Island, BC—he conveniently renamed after himself.

As Vancouver's ship sailed into this protected body of water, from his stance on the quarterdeck he saw dense conifers that furred the land, part of a five-thousand-year-old coastal rainforest that stretched from California to Alaska. Evergreen spires marched all the way down to the watery fringes of the rugged, hilly coastline, and white-mantled volcanoes loomed along the horizon. The trees that furred the coastal expanse included Sitka spruce upwards of 350 feet tall;[2] hemlock and true fir old growth grew in the elevations further inland. Through his spotting scope he saw an endless carpet of vegetable growth on steroids, a site he declared "luxurious."[3] The trees lived 200 to 1,000 years. It was like looking at a giant green pelt.

As he scanned the coastline, contrary to popular imagination, most of the trees he and his crew saw had been growing for only seventy years: a vast inferno, or family of fires, was said to have incinerated[4] the coastal areas in 1701. The flames, which occurred the year after a major megathrust earthquake, may have been intense enough to jump across Colvos Passage, a distance of .9 miles, from the current day Kitsap Peninsula to Vashon Island, as well as hop from shore onto many of the other puzzle-piece islands. The five-hundred-year-long Little Ice Age (1300 to 1850) brought extended drought, severe winter weather, and high wind to the region, all of which created windfalls and deadwood, enough to help ignite a massive scourge of orange and scarlet flames. Three to ten million acres of luxurious green rainforest burned. Although fire scar evidence shows up inland, many of the giants where I live—the Snoqualmie Valley--remained untouched.

The rampaging 1701 burn didn't mean that the trees near the coastline weren't large, they just weren't as large as they would become 150 years later as European settlement began in earnest. Fifty years after Vancouver mapped the area, explorer Charles Wilkes traveled on foot near the Nisqually River area (a river which sources from the southern flank of Mount Rainier and feeds into southern Puget Sound south of Tacoma, which gives an indication of how long the estuary is) and voyaged through a "gigantic fine cedar forest." Wilkes could not contain his astonishment regarding the impenetrable undergrowth between them, nor the way the trees thrust upward like cathedral spires. "Although they are sapplings (sic), [they] are six feet in diameter and upwards of 200 feet in height."[5]

Anywhere from half a billion to a billion trees would have covered the 6,300 square miles that surrounded the Salish Sea up to the lower foothills of the Olympics to the west, and the Cascades to the east. After the fire, which scorched an area more than the size of Denmark, Doug fir would have been one of the first successional trees to take root. Firs, with wood "remarkably fine" as described by Pliny the Roman naturalist, became the future old growth so valuable to the lumberjacks in the late 19th and early 20th centuries.

In 1853, to prepare the newly declared Washington Territory for settlement, the General Land Office began to set imaginary gridlines across the region, their corners marked with posts. Natural trees "witnessed" the grid corners and intersections. The "witness trees," though physically gone today, are recorded in early township archives, and help reveal what forest cover might have looked like even earlier, in pre-Columbian times. Although the average tree measured under nineteen inches, "one of every twenty-six pre-settlement trees was at least four feet across," trees that couldn't be embraced by two people with their arms spread out on either side. Roughly 2,500 to 5,000 of these very large trees grew in each square mile.[6] Some would have been close to three hundred years old; many were located north to south in the watersheds that spill from the Cascade's lip.

Settlers who came to the Snoqualmie Valley from New England, where forests had been depleted, must have felt they had entered a berserk green broccoli forest on growth hormones. A documentary calls this valley Land of the Giants. Situated over a large aquifer, the valley floor held a repository of rich mineral soil spilling out of the mountains, plentiful rain, and a mild climate. The tree trunks swelled to grain-silo size, visions of awe and beauty that produced cravings akin to dreams.

For thousands of years, people all over the world lived in what William Logan Bryant calls "creative engagement" with trees and plants. Bronze Age and Neolithic people pollarded trees in order to grow poles for structures, Mesa Verdeans bent fir trees to get limbs for lintels, and West Africans coppiced trees, which yielded them reliable fence materials to keep animals out, and grain and vegetables free to grow. In Europe, the practice of coppice and pollard had been well known and practiced for centuries, until the land barons came along and wanted pictorial landscapes, not functional ones. Where I live, and along the west coast, creative engagement had been in full swing for centuries. As Vancouver looked through his wooden and brass telescope, he might have glimpsed pockets of anthropogenic grasslands—maintained by Coast Salish clans for food gathering and game draws—that grew along what is now Belltown.

The Coast Salish culture contained, and still contains, an aspect called kinscape[7]: family clans, intermarriage, extended families, and relationships spread out over large distances. Kinscape implies landscape as part of the fabric of relationship, an apt word for people for whom trees are kin, especially the western red cedars, *Thuja Plicata*—of the cypress family. *Xpay'uhc* as they call it, provided everything the local Snoqualmie indigenous people needed, from cradles to canoes to coffins, and are called trees of life. With their feathered and braided flat needles hung with tiny bell-like cones, and silvery trunks composed of fine linear rows of bark, the cedars stand like elegant dowagers throughout the forest. They expand to twenty-six feet in diameter and can survive up to 1500 years. Their fibrous longitudinal bark, stripped from the tree using a method that produced a long triangle but didn't harm the tree, was woven into mats, baskets, and bowls. They split whole planks for houses off trees using wedges in a manner that kept the tree alive. When needed, the taking of a whole tree with an intentional "cut" using fire took many days, but the whole being was used: thin roots outside the canopy circle woven into baskets, layered bark pounded into flexible clothing, trunks carved into shelter, or transport. The tree supported them, and they in turn honored the tree with respect and prayers.

One hundred years after Vancouver, creative engagement began to come to an end. US President John Quincy Adams wanted the expanding republic "to make the wilderness blossom as the rose...to subdue the earth." I pull out *A History of the Snoqualmie Valley* from my backpack. While settlers put their farms on native prairies in order to avoid intensive clearing of trees, (and plowed up camas and potatoes cultivated by natives in the process), others turned to the lumber trade. Male pioneers, gripped with orgiastic visions of wealth, cut, sawed, and axed their way into a frenzy that left behind a bare, smoking, dirt-floored landscape, ugly and barren to the point of despair. The photos reveal flatbed rail cars loaded with logs as big in diameter as small ponds, stacked and waiting to depart the forest. One cedar tree—over twenty-eight feet in circumference—shown flanked by two men, reduces them to ants next to a coffee can. North Bend had its famous Maloney's Grove along the South Fork of the Snoqualmie River, with rented cabins and amusements, and having your photo taken on Maloney's fir stump, nine feet across and over six hundred years old, seemed a right-of-passage for those who visited.

Because loggers started their cuts above where the trunk flared into the ground, they left stumps capacious enough to be made into homes, barns, and even a post office. The most colossal tree in the book grew in the Milwaukee Railroad right of way in the upper valley—somewhere between Snoqualmie and North Bend. Fifty feet around at ground level, a group of men worked shifts, over 24 hours, to fell the magnificent ĉəbidac (pronounced che-*bee*-dotz), or Douglas fir. Eighty-four persons crowded onto the stump to pose for a photograph, with room for twenty more. The tree had been over a thousand years old; in its late middle-age, it could have thrived another five hundred years.

As commercial engagement replaced creative engagement, the trees seemed a never-ending supply of building materials to sell to a growing San Francisco to the south or shipped to places far flung as Hawaii. In the town where I live, originally called Tultxᵂ but now known as Carnation, they scraped all the trees off the valley floor, then set up intensive farming practices for hops and cattle; timber camps sprouted at Lake

Langlois, down at Griffin Creek, up Tolt Hill, and at Stillwater Hill in order to cut down the surrounding forest and create bare-naked hillsides. I imagine the trees as they succumbed to the ringing "misery whip" saws of the lumberjacks, as the great logs, defrocked of their massive branches (limbs that were themselves the diameter of trees), were skidded to the banks of the Tolt and Snoqualmie, floated downstream from forested slopes into the waiting arms of the sawmills. The source of all life here, our two rivers ended up carrying out their own dead, and then dying themselves, their waters silted by runoff and warmed by too much summer sun.

In Seattle, Yesler's Mill ran so long the tidal inlets on the Duwamish filled with sawdust, becoming known as Down on the Sawdust.[8] On most of the rivers that ran into Puget Sound, logging companies exploded rocks, broke up natural logjams from floods, and dammed up side channels which salmon used. They wanted fast water for floating timber. Here in the Snoqualmie Valley, twenty miles east of Yesler's mill, the denuded hillsides and bare riverbanks made the river a silted mess; with no logs to jam and slow the water for salmon fry, this meant faster, siltier water. Around the mill sites, the mountains of sawdust dumped into the water smothered salmon eggs and clogged the gills of dying fish.

The Snoqualmie, or sdukʷ albixʷ (pronounced roughly stuh-kwa-bew), and other indigenous peoples suffered many losses; perhaps the biggest one is loss of place, or loss of their "autochthonous rights" or the right to claim authentically to belong to this given area of forests, rivers, and abode of their ancestral spirits. By the early 1900's much of their land, stolen under the guise of federal treaties, lay in thrall to capitalism, and their beloved trees killed. I think of the modern day term solastalgia, which means a 'form of psychic or existential distress caused by environmental change.'[9] "The white men cut down all the great trees/And ran a railroad right through the land./Everyone was poor. Everyone helped everyone./I was midwife for my friend. And she was/midwife for me. We didn't give money to each other."[10] It's hard to imagine the distress they felt then, and feel today, caused by living in a kinscape-turned upside down, literally uprooted, from the ways they knew and still know.

What do these trees, the ones that remain, remember? Generations of indigenous placed their hands on their bark, hunted, prayed, buried their dead all around their feet or in their branches. Among their boughs, Douglas's squirrels or chicarees chattered and raised families; pileated woodpeckers and spotted owls nested in their cavities, and yellow-billed cuckoos and wood pigeons flocked throughout their canopies. I imagine the thousand-year-old tree in the photo, in this instance reduced to a flat gravestone of a stump, only multiplied. Over five thousand trees, some up to one thousand years old, all gone, reduced to discs spotting the ground like dinosaur footprints from here to the lip of the falls, and beneath the falls, throughout the lower valley where I live.

Today, the forests remain haunted by the ghosts of these giants. Many stumps, some still alive, are within walking distance of my home in the lower valley. The forest where I sit now, with the Mother tree nestled at my back, is dotted with them. Past and future intermingle, for often the deciduous ones like bigleaf maple have sprouted anew with fresh trunks that reach to the sky. If I'm haunted by the ghosts of the trees that once were, I'm drawn to those that escaped the misery whips, the steam donkey, and *Homo Sapiens Consumerii*. These aged trees are not paltry things. I'm entranced by these embattled, scarred survivors, maybe because I share their crenellated skin and rough, uncorked character of advanced age.

As I pack away my book and pull the rope from the Mother Tree, I think about how hard it is to imagine the diversity and density of the biomass contained in those ancient successional forests. One can get a narrow glimpse of how some forests may have looked in the deeper recesses of the middle fork of this same river: an understory thick with blowdowns, rotting logs, shelves of fungi ascending trunks, rills of tumbling water that feed into the river forks, an area rife with imagination, Bigfoot sightings, intense rainstorms, wildcats, bats, and owls. Mist and fog. But even there, it's mostly second growth.

What I longed to see was a forest of spirit. A forest—not just a single tree—that was like the old growth forests of old, where the trees grew large and fat like a stage set. As I stare off at a big stump with the characteristic springboard slots left by loggers, I think of the common forests in Europe, and of a book written by a German forest scientist, which argues, controversially--but only to a western mind--that plants are sentient, an idea shared by many cultures, and those of us who spend a lot of time in the outdoors. Ah, if only I knew a German forest scientist, I sniff.

I stand near Psilocybin Hill, looking southwest towards Paranoia Peak, somewhere near the Cascade crest and south of Interstate 90, close to the burble of Troublesome Creek. Fanged carnivores roam around these hills. It took an hour and a half drive in a utility truck on sewing-machine roads to get here, and rather than work the kinks out of our backs, we get out of the truck, walk through bear grass, burnt-orange tiger lilies, huckleberries, and piles of elk scat until we reach a tarn, or small mountain lake. Meadow grass surrounds the miniscule lake, and just beyond, mountain peaks rise straight up, covered with shaggy green spears of noble fir, Pacific Silver fir, mountain hemlock. To our left is a decayed log scratched open by an ant-seeking bear. We stand in a bowl of wilderness, two hors d'oeuvres on legs.

A tangible quiet pervades, punctured only by wing flaps, the buzzes of bees, dragonfly flybys, the audible swoops of swifts, and the whine of mosquitoes. Curtains of light hang over the bowl. A butterfly jitterbugs over the meadow; it's so quiet I hear it swallow. Annoyed squeaks rain down on us from a scree field above us, where picas, little rabbit cousins, make off-key notes as if blowing through duct-taped harmonicas. No human sounds exist here, save for our own thoughts.

That's because there are no cars allowed in this, the Cedar River Watershed, save for the vehicles of a handful of workers, spread over 600 miles of networked roads. No people allowed in here period--present company excluded. That means no hiking trails, nor any of the million hikers who inhabit Seattle, no pocketbook carrying, gum-chewing general public, no tourists Instagramming themselves while ignoring don't-pick-the-wildflower signs, no *Homo sapiens consumerii,* no rugged individualist overnight campers. And while we are at it, no serial killers, no oil lobbyists, no drunken inner-tube floaters. Miracle of miracles, even the logging companies have been thrown out. And because this unpeopled wilderness of 90,546 acres of forest, lakes, and rivers is a protected, gravity-fed, naturally filtered water supply for 1.5 million parched Seattleites, no human bodily functions allowed, either. Instead, there's thirty or more port-o-potties spread over miles that must be used no exceptions, should I--a writer with a hyped up endocrine system and a sprained foot--need to eliminate the gallon of coffee I drank on the way in to fix my caffeine-to-hemoglobin ratio. Fortunately for me, we passed one such *el banyo plastico* on the way up. It was so clean you could throw a dinner party inside.

What *is* here is old growth, high on the mountain tops. 14,000 delicious acres of it which my host has invited me to sample, but not before we gaze upon this diamond of a tarn. I'm mere miles from the upper plateau of my valley, less than thirty miles, as the heron flies, from my home. As we stare at the water the stillness feels as deep as the reflection of the mountains. Time measures itself in wing-beats here. It's so quiet, I find myself wondering if we are the last two people in the world and after I left home this morning all nuclear hell broke loose. Then my host's radio squawks, and I jump ten feet in the air.

This lovely, non-peopled wilderness, owned by the City of Seattle, has roughly forty-five employees. Many of them work on a road crew that, short of vacuuming and dusting the roads, makes sure there is no runoff, road sediment, or general crud which might contaminate the water supply. They track, measure, repair, buttress, study, and all but lick clean the byways in here, which are with minor exceptions, unpaved and thus permeable to water. Then there are the four to five staff who study and track the nature of this place, who try to understand what is going on with forest succession and lake ecology, and how it is changing. One of whom is my host, Rolf Gersonde, who happens to have been born and raised in West Berlin. A German forest scientist. An ecologist, to be precise.

I am here to help him take line transects of an old growth plot at 3,500 feet and hope I don't become a government experiment on how best to impale oneself on Devil's Club. Earlier, when I met him at the entrance gates, the Grimm's Fairy Tales part of my brain expected a roly-poly 80-year-old man with an axe over his shoulder. Mildly surprised by a 58-year-old athletic scientist with a waterproof iPad and the physique of someone who could climb the Matterhorn in fourteen minutes, the other thing I didn't expect this morning was a cliff.

The county I live in stretches from the coast to the Cascades, and resembles a trapezoid drawn by a drunken sawyer. Home to creatures as varied as seals, salmon, mountain goats, whales, and some rapidly melting glaciers, it's also home to 2,269,675 soggy, overcaffeinated humans, and six watersheds fed by the giant water collectors, the Central Cascades. The Cedar River Watershed's protected area is twice the size of a small European country. The protected part starts in meadows near the crest of the mountains, and becomes less protected, and more populated, as it spans the county west to the Salish Sea. Shaped like a banana, it includes 14 creeks, 3 lakes, and an inhabited island for the well-to-do. It includes Lake Washington which buffers us 'east-siders' from Seattle, a lake that represents a geographic social divide that Seattle-ites prefer never to cross.

My watershed—the Snoqualmie—intersects with this one, the Cedar River, in North Bend, just along Rattlesnake Lake. That was where Rolf picked me up earlier today at a set of double gates at 7:30 am, but not before I had technically committed a misdemeanor and eliminated some coffee behind some shrubs.

We cleared several electronic entrance gates and began our climb into the Cascades. As we zigzagged up forest service roads--left, right, switchback, ascent--the road diverged often enough I lost my sense of direction. Rolf didn't consult any maps--this place was mapped on his heart, a small world he knew really well, but a world, too, he told me this morning in his low, gentle cadence, of responsibility, of good stewardship of the land.

"We have a mandate from the people. I'm not doing this for myself."

A stunning, long blue lake appeared, embedded in the forest below. We drove alongside it for what seemed like a long time. The lake's real name, Nooknu, means *place where the water gathers*. In 1889 after Seattle suffered a devastating fire, some enterprising folks wanted to create a water supply for the city. They focused on this natural groundwater lake, and installed a masonry dam, which drowned some forest and several small towns, before it created the much larger Chester Morse Lake, which took the shape of a long, blue multi-pronged ghost. The water, by the time it left here, was screened, chlorinated, fluoridated, ozonated, disinfected, and supplemented with lime to prevent lead-pipe leaching. But inside the watershed protection zone it was still wild, tinged with moss and stone. Ralph stopped the truck at a roadside cascade pouring over some mossed rocks. He has imbibed the water from this natural spring for ten years.

"Of course, you take your own risk," he quipped with a grin as he jumped into the gully and held the container under the rill.

As we ascended the twisted ridges, the lanes grew more primitive, and the forest grew younger. Before logging was discontinued, each drainage had been logged west to east, except for the tops of the mountains and high ridges, which the logging companies couldn't reach. That's where most of the old growth lived now. He stopped the truck and pointed to a ridge across the lake. About 1/3 of the way down the ridge, he indicated with a wave of his hand where a dark band of trees, a ragged layer of Noble and Pacific fir lived. The trees had broken, rebuilt crowns, and bore signs of a lifetime of insect infestation, heavy snow loads, winds, and disease. Their greenery looked patched and clumped. Old growth.

The raggedness of these trees, he explained, was part of the interplay of an old growth forest, "the building and restoring that the forests do as a whole." He pointed to another layer just below the old growth, where the trees rose in perfect, symmetrical spears: second growth. Then he put the truck in gear.

As the truck climbed the road, I ask him how he ended up here, in this little corner of the US. When Rolf was young, he often spent time in West Berlin's parks by himself, but his family also valued outdoorsmanship; later, after college, he ended up working for the forest industry in Washington, amidst concerns about forest declines in Europe, and acid rain on the East Coast. In 1998 he earned a degree from UC Berkeley, in Environmental Science Policy and Management, then got hired by the watershed. He and his wife have lived in North Bend, in the upper Snoqualmie Valley, ever since. His wife ran a well-stocked, popular general store near Rattlesnake Lake, where Rolf also sold used mountaineering books and literature on the outdoors. I knew it well.

We continued to bump and rise in elevation. Rolf took left and right forks without slowing, while I followed on my map. The watershed was a place of beauty and almost military-style surveillance: down by Rattlesnake Lake, a computer tracked our location. In case of a rollover, or accident, they could find us, or if we went AWOL, which is what I'd like to do.

This part of the watershed, like all the watersheds in the county, had been in continuous use by various indigenous groups for hunting, gathering, and vision quests. As we neared the Cascade crest and made a hairpin turn, I asked where the original footpath over the mountains was (it's not where I-90 cuts through the pass). Rolf pointed down below us to an inviting meadow dotted with evergreens, where he believed the ancient pathway, still visible in some places, existed. Soon the road turned up and south. On our right the forest grew dense and dark. The boles, tightly packed together, resembled a forest drawn in charcoal pencil, no sunlight, no understory; just a dark, uninviting woodland. This was what second growth looked like up close; most hikers encountered similar patches within the Cascades. It looked barren. "The loggers removed all the slash and deadfall; with no slash, there's no understory. When they burned the slash it became a homogenous seedbed, a monoculture of about 1,000 trees per acre."

He gestured out his window to the opposite side of the road, which they had thinned to mimic a more natural environment, as if it hadn't ever been logged: huckleberry, Devils club, red flowering currant, ferns, vanilla leaf, and mosses made a green undulating carpet in between trees. The deciduous foliage dropped off each fall, provided micro-nutrients to the soil, and built up organic matter. The plants provided 15-25% of the nutrients the trees needed, and helped the forest grow up. It also made better habitat for insects, for birds to fly through and forage in, and for browse for deer and elk and myriad mammal species. "We thinned this area down to about 400 trees per acre, but in some cases that's not good enough." To look back and forth from the lush side to the dark, barren upright trunks on the other, was a contrast in ideologies.

As if to prove his point we startled a Barred Owl perched near the road. The owl made several short, twisted flights around the dark boles to our right in the barren ugly forest, then spied on us from a branch. "It's not easy for the owl to navigate through that thicket of trunks, but he'll still hunt in there if he has to."

Which brings me to the heavily forested cliff Rolf has just parked alongside of. After we left the peacefully quiet tarn, we drove a quarter mile back down the road. At the bottom of the cliff, in a steep forested bowl, lies one of a hundred plus forest plots he studies. Every ten years he and a small crew measure various things within each plot; it takes them three years to collect information from all the plots. Before we hop out and don our backpacks he turns and says with a glint in his eye:

"It's time to turn the forest into numbers."

In the truck bed: an odd assortment of PVC pipes, wires, a utility bucket, pieces of metal. It looks like we are about to build a satellite. He starts pulling pipes out— some have black, red, and white increments marked on them, others are blank. He hands me two six-foot sections—"You can use these as hiking sticks," he says half joking in accented English, then picks up the rest and points to where we are going: through a line of thick trees and boulders, straight down into the ravine. Or cliff. There's no clear way to get through the line of trees, and no way to know if the route you've chosen will result in a good descent. His pale blue eyes narrow as he smiles.

"At some point, you just need to commit," he laughs as we walk along the edge of the road, and with that, he disappears through the scrub. Between the terrain and the predators, I'm glad he showed me where the keys to the truck are kept. Rolf is almost a third of the way down the slope before I fight my way through the line of trees and boulders—I'm only five foot one--and start to descend into the north-facing ravine. I follow him down, sprained foot and all, as he hops over blow downs, balances on downed trees, crunches through huckleberry and ferns up to our necks, until we stop near the bottom of a green bowl of forest.

He's looking for markers—flagging, PVC pipes sticking out of the ground, or worse, bare rebar, which delineates the transect line. Bare rebar? I'm informed it's poking up out of the ground all over—invisible of course in forest duff—but most notably on the downed tree bole I'm balancing on. Lucky for me, some rebar is covered by white PVC pipes, and pink flagging marks others. Rolf thrashes around to find the center of the 70-meter measurement area. He crunches back and we dump the gear and pipes in a small clearing.

Rolf dons a vest with pockets, loops a stylus around his neck, and tucks a hammer into a pocket sewn into the vest's back. Until he gets his transect lines set up and his first set of measurements entered into his iPad, he tells me I'm free to "get to know the forest." While he approximates the canopy cover with a small, curved mirror marked with grid lines, fitted into his palm, I stand in a patch of sun under a canopy opening.

In this north-facing ravine, shocks of light pour onto the forest floor, and Greeklike columns of silver trunks thrust skyward to stupefying heights. The canopy holds its palms up towards invisible stars. Looking north through the forest I see bright sun-plashed meadows. The air looks and smells green. Here, time acts more like brightness or loudness, more magnitude than currency.

Far below the treetops, I swim in a leafy sea. Huckleberry bushes grow over my head, and I could drown in the clumps of sword fern, some of which grow to Carboniferous proportions. I thrash around for a while, then work my way over to a clearing, past knee-high shrubs of silver fir. At my feet, False hellebore, with its large curvilinear emerald leaves and poisonous black rhizomes, sprouts from a moist seep on the forest floor, and a host of vanilla leaf with their tri-leaf patterns forms a herd of little moose heads around my ankles. Myriad ferns stick up like green feather dusters, and though it's early August, at this elevation the lime green of new growth or spring fir tips--which make a bracing tea--remain visible on little fir seedlings. The pendulous cones of Pacific Silver Fir *(Abies amabilis)* Grand Fir *(Abies grandis)* and Douglas Fir *(Pseudotsuga menziesii)* litter the ground in armloads. Half-discs of artist fungus or bear bread stick out from dead trees. I thrash back into the understory, then submerge: down on my hands and knees I smell dark mold, imagine roots gently probing the soil.

Bees and wasps and horseflies zip around, their wings ablur. From the forest edge comes the "quick THREE beers" of an Olive sided flycatcher, hawking for insects. Then the descending vee-eer call of nighthawks, a bird shaped like a little boomerang usually heard at dusk. In the ancient quiet, I hear sunlight filtering through the canopy, the whine of mosquitoes, fungus growing, elk scat decaying. I hear the plink of fir needles as they fall every few moments like rain. Intermittently, I hear Rolf crunching around like the bear that I joked earlier will come and eat him, and leave me stranded, hopefully for the rest of my life.

I resurface, walk over to where we left our gear, and slowly swivel my head around like an owl to look at this patch of old growth woodland. I don't want to tell Rolf, but I'm disappointed. These aren't the fat boles of old growth I was expecting. I've been spoiled by my verdigris fantasies of what used to thrive on the valley floor, the tantalizing photographs of ancient diverse stands made obese by a diet of water by the ton, and alluvial minerals by the mountain-load. I wanted woods like Vancouver and Wilkes saw, what the Coast Salish people knew, woods that held multilayered canopies like green clouds and trunks big around as a circus tent. Here the old growth looks....dare I say, skinny. The trees, around 350 years old, started out life during the Little Ice Age. At this altitude, above 3,000 feet, they live on an anorexic diet of long winters, cool summers, and lack the alluvial soil and volumes of water that their cousins in the lowlands have in abundance. Their trunks look thin. Though they lack the buttressed bases and width of age you'd see on the valley floor, some of the trees can grow to a thousand years old or more. Each tree wears a silver numbered tag: with their dangling earrings, they are the arboreal equivalent of aging supermodels.

Rolf finishes his first set of survey data. We have a snack (carrots for him, chocolate for me, revealing deeply held priorities). Then he takes four pipes and fits them into a 4' x 4' square, and I discover what all this rebar is for: he attaches one corner of the square to the rebar that sticks up along the transect line. Within each quadrant, we measure and estimate percentages of moss, herbs, and shrubs. Rolf calls out the four-letter species codes, and as I enter them into the iPad, the plants begin to separate into distinct individuals, each square of leafy vegetation revealing a world of delicate beings.

The maroon spires of the saprophytic Western coralroot, which lacks the ability to make its own food and depends on decaying organic matter to survive; two different kinds of huckleberry, distinguishable by subtle variations in leaf shape and taste; Queens cup lilies, with their ovate leaves sticking out of the ground in a whorl, their single white starshaped flowers already come and gone, and the clustered leaves of Dwarf bramble, whose berries are said to "miniaturize the essence of raspberry flavour (sic) as perfectly as wild strawberries do the essence of strawberry."[11] There's Rosy Twisted-stalk, with its long arching unbranched stem, though I have to imagine its little rose and white flower bells, and Five-leaved bramble or creeping raspberry, whose five leaves resemble a toe-print.

Nothing goes unremarked: leaf litter, rocks, moss, plants, even decaying tree trunks noted and measured for their rate of decline. I feel a marked sense of renewal helping to attend to the details of identification, the sparse fringes of hair at the nodes, whether a stalk is slender or fat, or a leaf shiny or matte, and whether the flowers have produced berries yet. If some plants were strangers to me, even as I reduce them to percentages in a square, a kinship develops just in the act of looking, of noticing, as if I were now at a reunion of friends. All the foliage is flecked and glistening with sugar from the aphids high above us sucking on the tree canopy.

Rolf has looked at historic photographs of various parts of this watershed in detail. His observations reveal that what stays relatively static at a larger scale—old trees, young trees, understory species—remains, at a smaller scale, very dynamic. Trees live in a different time scale than their frenetic, watch-obsessed human counterparts: two thirty has as much meaning here as a pair of cufflinks. If you could look at a forest through time lapse photography, and condense one hundred years down to a minute, you'd see vegetation and trees growing and decaying in rapid jerk-filled movements. But viewed through a human lens, trees appear sloth-like.

In this sea-light, surrounded by this grove of jewelry-obsessed supermodels who move in their own time zone, a strange flicker of thought washes over me. If relation is mutual, if, as Ellen Meloy writes, kindship demands reciprocity, it occurs to me that maybe the plot is measuring us, not vice versa. What kind of awareness, I wonder, do the plants carry of us, as we move along with our quadrant, careful not to step on any?

Over lunch (fancy cheese sandwich with greens for him, squashed peanut butter for me), Rolf tells me how the field of ecology—objective science--defines an old growth forest. It has to have been primary forest, having never been harvested and therefore relatively free of human interference. It has to be in 'late seral stage' where trees like Doug fir are gradually replaced by silver fir and hemlock. And my personal favorite, it has to have decadence. By decadence, Rolf refers to the standing dead trees that have come to the end of their natural lifespan, and the decaying logs necessary for regeneration of new life. I love the word: my mind flashes on trees shooting heroin, robbing convenience stores, and driving into the city in logging trucks so they can fall on people. Rolf's point: while some second growth trees are bigger in diameter than some of the old growth here, this plot contains something second growth stands lack; a complexity and thus a stability that begins to come into partial view when you turn the forest into numbers.

As I sit in the coolness, I feel the interconnectedness and the quiet wonders of this place. Beyond the plant communities, the architecture of old growth—shaggy, clumped crowns, tops that become more rounded, deadfalls that create openings, help a host of wildlife to thrive: bats can glide through openings in branches and canopy, owls can hunt more freely. Truffles thrive in the old mycorrhiza, which are eaten by flying squirrels, who are in turn eaten by spotted owls. Insects love the crevices and messiness in which they hide, breed, and hunt. The canopy shelters Swainsons thrushes, while the lower reaches of trunks, with cavities and crevasses, create homes for red squirrels, or chicarees. Little teacup wrens live in the foliage lower down. The web of connection unfolds a map wide in all directions: the marbled murrelet flies twenty miles inland from the Salish Sea to lay a single egg in a depression on the wide, lichened branches of old growth; it will fly out to the sea to feed, and comes back at night to incubate its brown-flecked orb. Science only 'discovered' the marbled murrelet's nesting habits recently. What else don't we understand?

The tangled thickets of sword fern are food for the mountain beavers, living fossils who dig holes in the soft soil with their Yoda-like fingers and live under tree roots near seeps and streams. Banana slugs cruise the dense floor, turning dead leaves and animal feces into a glistening rich soil. And, of course, as we breathe out, the trees breathe in, and turn carbon dioxide into oxygen.

As we eat and talk, surrounded by hordes of vanilla leaf, used indoors for its vanilla scent, and Indian hellebore, or Corn Lilly, a "violently poisonous" plant, used for a variety of medicinal uses, I think of this plot, what Rolf calls a reference condition or reference plot. Rolf tries to make sense of what's happening here. Most of the forest in the watershed is mid-seral or 70-80 years old, and as he explains, they want it to move into the late seral stage. In other words, how does a second growth forest, decimated by logging and devoid of what a forest needs, like the dark forest by the roadside we passed earlier, develop complexity and stability like the one we're sitting in? Surrounded by traditional medicinal plants, and trees that provide shelter, it's hard not to think of the older lifeways as those that guide us towards those two things— complexity, stability--lifeways that were scraped away just like forest duff during the European land scramble of the past 170 years.

We finish our sandwiches and take up the quadrant again, moving east along the transect line. In the vespertine light, the sounds of birdsong and insect wings, no longer plangent, become woolly, as if we're underwater. I feel myself edging into bottle-green torpor as we wade through shrubs that resemble green spindrift. I've breathed in so many phytochemicals I feel high.

The hours tick by, and the sun trickles through different parts of the canopy in the late afternoon. The supermodels with their frothy skirts of understory have a narcotic effect; time loosens from its strictures. We take a walk around, for the old growth extends far beyond the plot lines. We tiptoe among the plants towards a ravine, where a stream meanders, fed by the little tarn we visited. Taking careful steps, Rolf explains he likes to see what else is here, outside the boundaries of the transect lines, and I can tell he enjoys the respite from percentages, from objectivity. Surprises abound. He points out this or that plant, then he tells me there could be orchids. These are not the showy hothouse supermarket floozies in Trader Joe's. They are subtle, tiny.

What's this, I ask, pointing to a thin green fuzzy stick less than a foot high, with pale green yellow flowers dotting its top half. They look less like flowers than little traps. Up close, very close, there are horn-like teeth at the base of each trap. "Well, hello there," he says to the plant. An orchid. The orchid is likely a Northwestern Twayblade, or *Listera caurina*. It's a stick with attitude: some twayblades blow their pollen out explosively so as to glue it to unsuspecting insects. It occurred to me that this is the poetry of survival, a forest of spirit. And also, the precious little things—stems that sneeze pollen—that the logging companies decimate when they "harvest" a forest, and that developers in the lowlands kill when they raze land to erect giant box-like homes.

Too soon, we have to go, so we gather the pipes and gear and hike back up the cliff. Surprisingly we emerge close to the truck. I ask if he can take me back to the little tarn before we leave, knowing I may never see this place again. He agrees, of course, and we drive back up. The bowl lies bathed in golden light, the tarn at its center like earth's green eye. As we wander, we find mosquito larval casings left as high-water marks on a rock by the lake, and walk through violets. The band of pikas shriek at us again. The sun lights up a meadow behind the trees, halfway up the mountain beyond; it casts the opening in a buttery light: a hidden meadow, invisible in this morning's sun, now visible, but out of reach like a dream.

As Rolf guides the truck downhill on the graveled byways, he tells me that many years ago he began conversations with some economists about the ecological system services that the Cedar River Watershed provides. The economists did some analysis and discovered that the intrinsic benefits to humans, or the non-monetary values, outstripped the value of the forest as extractive goods. As he explains it, the 'existence value' of this place also has emotional value, and the economists were able to put a price tag on it.

I nod in agreement as the blur of green rolls by the windows. It reminds me of the way the Coast Salish think when they speak about the emotional pricelessness of their ancestral lands. We come around a bend and a fat marmot sits by the side of the road, then flies up in the air. We've discovered a new species: a winged forest-marmot. But no. It's another barred owl. Around another turn, we startle three ruffed grouse, who scramble up into the undergrowth.

He unhooks the radio and lets the central office know we'll be out soon—everyone has to be out of the watershed by 6 pm. He squints as we head into a sunlit portion of road, one hand on the wheel.

"Nowadays expectations are different. We call that the "shift in baseline." When my daughter, who is 17, was born, we used to see people lined up all along the Lake Washington bridge into Seattle, fishing for sockeye. Since 2006 we haven't seen that.

My daughter won't know what it's like. Today, tree mortality is common. People get used to things being the way they are, because they don't remember any other way."

In other words, since all of our thousand-year-old trees, the ones that diminished us to the size of ants, have mostly been cut down (and to see one today takes effort), people don't miss their presence.

What am I in search of when I seek old trees? When I look at old photos of gigantic boles, so fat they reduce humans to miniscule specks, I'm seized with a nostalgia I cannot name. Perhaps because these trees, with their Hollywood-on-steroids, Jack-and-the-Beanstalk size, dwarf any human endeavor. When we lived in and among large plants, life had the grace that humility brought, and the giants reminded us of wonder.

Lately, the cadre of man-children who rule Silicon Valley have determined that the human race should ride in self-driving cars, live in a metaverse rather than reality, and worse, go live on Mars. One toxic capitalist wizard has declared that life on other planets will be necessary in order to preserve human "consciousness." Man has become so afraid of nature he requires whole planets between him and greenery. Never mind that gravity is essential to having skeletal systems that function, and that greenery and nature is part of the poetry of our survival, Silicon Valley envisions us better off as withered, gelid hominids staring into screens while sitting in a barren landscape at -80 Fahrenheit. These scenarios also neglect that with our precious "consciousness," we will be the first species to witness our own extinction.

I'd rather clothe myself in cedar bark and goat hair, eat dried huckleberry cakes, make vessels out of fine roots and grasses than to go live on Mars. When I can't face humanity's inane antics anymore, I slither out the door before my own skeleton turns into jelly and my brain descends into blubber-brained insanity, and return to the old technologies: my legs, a pen, a notebook. I return to the Mother Tree at the Twin Falls trail.

Rolf knows this tree as well, he thinks it's a fine old tree, and he agreed with my age assessment of at least five hundred years, which pleased me. Of Susan Simard's work, he believes it is groundbreaking. I lean my back against the Mother tree's flaky skin and place my derriere back over the mining operation. Simard aptly points out that above and below ground, a forest has the same pattern as a neural network; some of the compounds that trees exchange, are the same as some neurotransmitters in the human brain.

While trees may not have a brain, she says, "Plants perceive, receive information, and make decisions. They have memories. They can learn. These are all attributes we ascribe to intelligence...all those abilities and skills evolved over hundreds of millions of years." And while humans "came along much later in evolutionary history...the origin of [tree and plant] intelligence is much more complex and not that much different than we find in human beings."[12]

Science cautions us against anthropomorphizing. It's even, according to many in the white male echelon that has dominated the genre, the big 'no-no' of nature writing. But for a species built on stories, we require metaphors. I can't help but think that metaphors bring us into equality with the world. They allow us to imagine beyond our rigid scientific definitions, to other possibilities, to acknowledge that, yes, trees have intelligence. This is how the First Nations people view trees, and how Greek philosophers did, like Pliny the Elder, who attributed sense, and spirit, to plants.

All I know this morning, as I sit with my back up against the tree with my eyes closed is this: while I can help turn a forest into numbers to better understand its lifeways, the language of numbers only takes humans so far. My childhood, steeped as it was in the language of science, lacked words to describe the mysteries and awe I felt in a forest. While the *Life Nature Library* series my father owned had opened the door to nature for me as a child, science, with its insistence on dry theoretical frameworks, fell woefully short for me on imagination. Imagination marches right up to the borders of science, and occasionally, bursts through, as when Simard wondered if trees nurtured instead of competed.

Many indigenous cultures combine imagination with deep knowledge, reflected in their language, such as the Potawatomi word *puhpowee*, which describes "the force which causes mushrooms to push up from the earth overnight."[13] Potawatomi Nation member Robin Wall Kimmerer's question in *Braiding Sweetgrass*, what if nature loves us back? is the reciprocal part of the poetry of survival. We've forgotten we are a part of something that provides for us: bacteria that keep us alive live in our gut and on our skin; trees that provide oxygen, wood for houses, and food to eat. The loss we incur after the land of the giants has been all cut down is the loss of what makes us human: the love we would have gotten if we treated nature right, if we allowed nature to love us back. To turn a tree into a 'thing,' or a forest into numbers, is to obfuscate what it is: kith and kin.

In my numerous visits to the Mother Tree, I've never seen her crown. My observations stopped at the point where her main leader had cracked off, leaving the jagged impression she was in decline. I assumed the green boughs I saw near her top were from the trees around her, or were other species living off her decay. I decide to take a better look. I amble through the understory fifty feet in various directions, and glass her crown from different vantage points, against a backdrop of birdsong and the susurrus of the South Fork.

A fat bole rises another thirty feet into the sky beyond the cracked off part. A number of branches and greenery adorn her top. I zoom in on one of the green boughs and bring the foliage into focus. The whorls of needles go all the way around the stem. Not flat, like hemlock. Definitely Doug fir.

The Mother Tree is alive.

Endnotes

[1] It's a case study in why we need more women (as well as people of color) in science: people with different cultural experiences, such as Native Americans, have life experiences that exist well outside the dominant societal, religious, cultural, political, and scientific, "norm," so they naturally, with their different life experiences, ask different questions than the standard, lab-coated white guys.

[2] Seattle Times Staff, "Giant Logged Long Ago, Not Forgotten," *The Seattle Times*, September 4, 2011, updated September 5, 2011, https://www.seattletimes.com/life/giant-logged-long-ago-but-not-forgotten/.

3 "II. Seeing the forest for the Trees: Placing Washington's Forests in Historical Context," Center for the Study of the Pacific Northwest, University of Washington, Accessed April 4, 2022, https://www.washington.edu/uwired/outreach/cspn/Website/Classroom%20Materials/Curriculum%20Packets/Evergreen%20State/Section%20II.html.

4 Tom Schroeder, Pre-Settlement Forests Around Puget Sound: Eyewitness Evidence, April 22, 2022, https://www.biorxiv.org/content/10.1101/592733v5.

5 "Seeing the Forest for the Trees."

6 "Pre-settlement Forests Around Puget Sound."

7 Word from *Over the Falls* by Jay Miller, usage mine.

8 Murray Morgan, "One Man's Seattle" in *Skid Road*, Revised edition, (New York: Viking Press, 1960), Page 9.

9 Robert McFarland, "The Edge" in *Underland*, (New York: W.W.Norton & Company, Ltd, First American Edition, 2019) p. 317.

10 Patrick Twohy, "At Home No Longer" in *Beginnings, A Meditation on Coast Salish Lifeways,* (LaConnor, WA: Patrick Twohy, Second Edition 2003), p. 64. The quote is from Marya Moses, Snohomish.

11 Jim Pojar, Andy MacKinnon, *Plants of the Pacific Northwest Coast: Washington, Oregon, British Columbia & Alaska,* compiled and edited by Pojar and MacKinnon (Canada: BC Ministry of Forests and Lone Pine Publishing, 1994) p. 79.

12 Susan Simard, *Treeline: The Secret Life of Trees,* (directed by Jordan Manley, produced by Laura Yale and Monika McClure), Patagonia Films, January 27, 2019, film on YouTube, accessed September 12, 2023, https://www.youtube.com/watch?v=YCEaYInJbos.

13 Robin Wall Kimmerer, "Learning the Grammar of Animacy" in *Braiding Sweetgrass*, (Minneapolis: Milkweed Editions, 2013), p. 49.

On the Wing
Cypseloides niger (Black Swift)

Angela Waldie

Stay on the trail:
leave the swifts to their secret cave
in misted echo of mountain water

two nests, or three, or four
where once were twelve

each shelters a single chick
through a season of cliffs,
a brief communion with stone

before they learn to feed in air
make love in air, roost in air

descend to slick canyons
only in summer
to shelter those who cannot fly

until they learn to follow
storms for swarms of insects
fly higher than sight
on clear days,
higher than knowledge

to still elude
maps that shatter mystery
spend summers in hidden canyons
winters far aloft

to dream in air
and on nights when the moon is full
to soar above its light

honing this dance
with darkness, absence, distance, flight.

Asemic Text w347

Gregory Stump

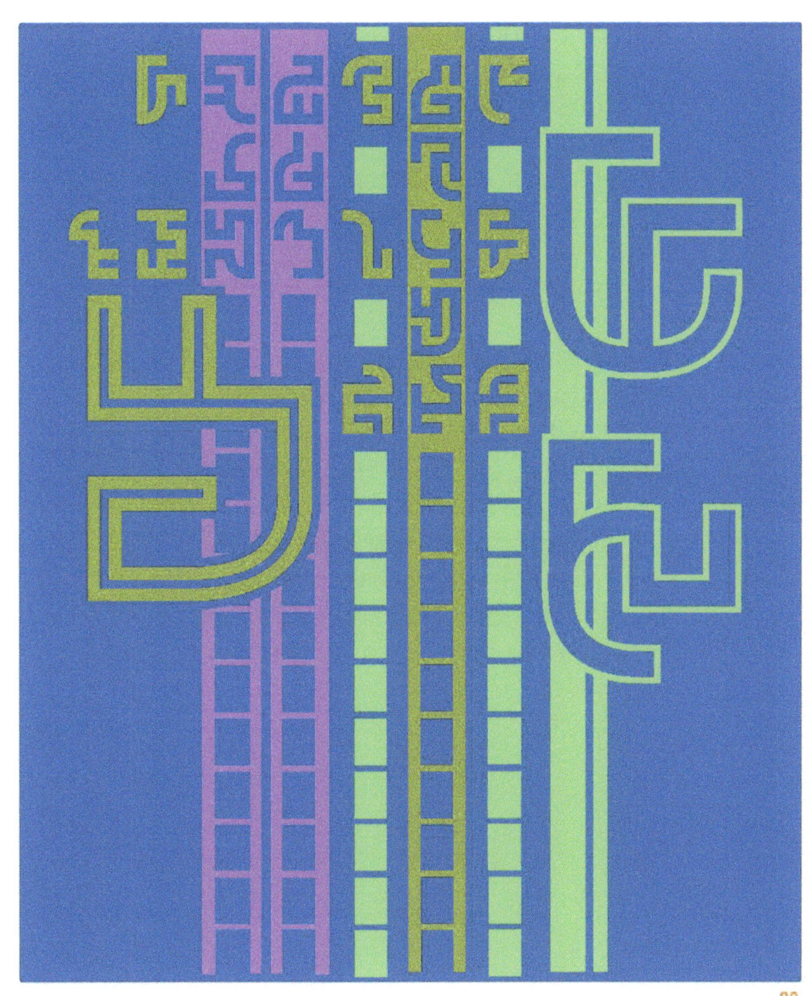

Feathers and Catkins
Betula occidentalis (River Birch)

Angela Waldie

River birch, teach me to grow
wild by a frozen river,
limbs outstretched to welcome winter,
feathered by silence and snow.

Sunlight stored in crisp, brown catkins,
seeds like counterweights to sorrow.
Whatever I take from Earth is borrowed.
Let me grow wild by a frozen river.

Limbs outstretched to welcome redpolls,
I bend beneath their gentle shivers.
Feel the hope that wings deliver
winter's counterweights to sorrow.

Let the snow fall deep tomorrow.
Offer sunlight stored and borrowed
and all the hope that wings deliver.
Teach me to grow by a frozen river.

Going All In

Katrina Irene Gould

On September 9 of 2022, I drove through forests devoured by fire. Two years earlier, white-hot fingers of lightning swept across central Oregon. Where the lightning found tinder in the summer-dry branches, cones, and needles of pine and fir trees, the Beachie Creek and Lionshead fires were born. When a historic windstorm joined the fray, it drove the fires on faster, pushing them toward each other. The wind buoyed the flames, enabling them to leap from one tree top to the next. Fire boiled through blackened trees sending oily smoke into the air. Think of a bedsheet on a clothesline billowing like a sail, folding in on itself, snapping the edges, rippling and whipping. Now, imagine that same bedsheet in a garish, greasy reddish-orange conflagration.

My daughter, her boyfriend, and I drove through lodgepole pines, cedars, and mountain hemlocks destroyed by these fires. We planned to meet my husband and son for a last-minute camping trip during the new moon. They'd headed up the North Santiam Corridor early on a Friday, planning to snag a walk-in site for the weekend. The rest of us worked until five o'clock. We drove a second car, expecting a phone call letting us know where our scouts had finally landed.

Our ultimate destination was Malheur County at the far eastern edge of Oregon. Friday, we'd get to the Jefferson Wilderness Area, and drive the longest leg on Saturday. We'd been away from this area since the fires had incinerated several small towns and flamed through more than 200,000 acres of forest - an area a quarter the size of Rhode Island. Signs of the devastation began before we reached Mill City. Then, as we gained altitude, blackened trees dotted the hillsides like chemo hair. This evidence of vulnerability filled me with a sickening grief and a strange sense of humiliation.

I've lived long enough that I expect Nature to change, but I also hope for a certain predictability as well. I had driven this route at least once every year of my adult life. Mill City was meant to be secluded from the highway, tucked behind an impenetrable thicket of Douglas fir, juniper, and maple trees across the North Santiam River. It wasn't meant to be laid bare, exposed to the stream of cars on the highway. Tears started in my eyes, and I was grateful my daughter and her boyfriend sat up front.

My phone rang. "We found a beautiful spot," my son raved.

We took the turnoff from Highway 22 and followed the Breitenbush River. The waning light saturated the greens of returning foliage, as well as the ashy silvers and charcoal blacks of trees whose sap had boiled until they died. The remaining plants and trees, alive and dead, showed the route the fire had taken. Here, it jumped the river, there, it left an inexplicable swath untouched; here, the dead, black trees stood ramrod straight, there, only the canopy appeared singed. Who could understand the reasoning of fire?

I had a hold of my emotions by the time we turned into the campground. Many campgrounds since Mill City had been closed, and though this one was open, rangers had roped off several sites with yellow danger tape. The fire had made its way through here, too, deciding to spare some campsites and not others.

Our site lay on the river side of the grounds. The parking pull-off and the actual campsite were separated by a short path through vine maple and Doug fir, thick with thigh-high clusters of sword fern. We walked toward the sound of the river.

Bags of food covered the picnic table. On the far stretch of one bench, someone had perched our cooler, and our tent sat beyond that, already pitched in front of a rickety-looking split rail fence. Garth, my exuberant husband, threw his arms wide to greet us.

"The river is right there," I said, delighted it was so close.

"Isn't it great?" my son agreed.

On the other side of the fence, eighty feet down and already in shadow, flowed the river. Up river, the water created a stairway, then, as it neared the banks directly below me, the steps flattened out, and shallower areas ran smooth for several yards. Stones of turquoise, rust, and white glistened beneath the surface, visible even from this height, even in shadow. Downstream, the river spread into a wide bowl, held by the steep slope on the opposite bank – a perfect swimming hole.

"Do you want to go down?" Garth asked.

I was tired and cranky from the drive, and the miles of charred forest. "No. I'll wait."

I turned back toward the river. Along this stretch, it cut a distinct line. Summer greenery flourished on our side with hundred-year-old trees sporting dusty, dark-green needles. On the other side, Douglas firs loomed, silvered and blackened from the wildfire and stripped of growth. At their base, returning maidenhair ferns, sprightly poplars, and oxalis hugged the ground. Those trees not entirely destroyed by fire drooped like stroke victims, green on one side, and shiny gray on the other. Several dead trees lay jumbled in the river.

Our tent was big enough for three, but my son and husband each wanted to sleep under the stars. Not me. Stars were great, but I needed sleep, which meant feeling contained by walls, even if they were only made of nylon. I tucked my glasses into the corner pocket of the tent. The sound of the river filled the night air and I let myself fall into sleep.

We planned, the next morning, after a leisurely start, to pack up and head on the five-hour drive to our destination. I drank an unhurried cup of coffee and ate a bowl of oatmeal. The soft, summery air discouraged haste, and bid us lounge instead. We lazed for one hour, then two, and the temperature rose. Finally, Garth said, "We need to start thinking about going."

Our son slumped further into his chair, the picture of relaxation. "I'm happy to start *thinking* about it," and we laughed.

I leveraged myself out of the sagging camp chair. "Okay. I need to visit the river first."

"Can I come, too?" Garth hopped off the bench.

"Sure." I shrugged.

I would've been wiser to learn from my birthday experience. I'd undertaken a summer project, to put my feet in waters that flowed from mountain rivers and streams whenever possible. I hiked along the Salmon River on my sixty-first birthday. I planned to wade in and see what happened. But I couldn't figure out how to commune with the river while my fellow hikers stood around, trying not to look restless. I hadn't thought this far ahead. Sweat gathered beneath my bra straps and encircled my waist and thighs where my underpants gathered. Finally, I gave up, unable to lose my self-consciousness.

Garth and I skittered down a slurry of stones and forest detritus. Silty dirt and pebbles carpeted the roots and small outcroppings of basalt that stretched across the path, making the steep slope all the more treacherous. Eventually, the path leveled out and ended on the rocky beach below our tents.

Two winters' worth of debris littered the ground. Sharp stubs of branches jutted from the fallen logs. I steadied myself on Garth and removed my hiking boots and socks, then rolled up my jeans and waded in. The water was cold, but not glacial. The hard stones hurt my feet. I stagger-walked in deeper and stood in the flow.

The river gurgled and sparkled. The sunlight beamed from behind the opposite bank above the steeply rising dead trees. I waited, but couldn't attune to the river while Garth stood by, patient and respectful, but present nonetheless. Whatever I would have done had he not been there - chant? skinnydip? see a fairy? shout my creed? - lay beneath a burden of inhibition.

I felt demoralized, shifting back and forth on my aching feet. I cupped handfuls of water and bathed away sticky sweat from my arms. I wiped another refreshing handful across the back of my neck. Then I straightened. I'd come to the river, hoping some affinity would emerge, and now I didn't know what I was even supposed to be feeling. I'd submerged my feet as planned; maybe that was enough?

Growing up female in America, one learns to think of herself as a person *looked at.* Childhood's unselfconsciousness allows her mind to be with itself without always including others. Soon enough, though, she can't escape wondering, *How will it look to them for me to do this?* Like bleeding to death from the proverbial thousand cuts, my presence in the world gave way, more and more, to an awareness of myself as an observed and evaluated being. More and more, I lost touch with my own agenda, increasingly incapable of shutting out the agendas of others.

I breathed hard as we scrabbled up the path. We needed to strike camp and drive till dinnertime. It was why we were here, but I couldn't stir up much enthusiasm.

While we were gone, the other campers had decided we should *not* get back in the cars. Instead, they proposed we stay a second night. It was the easiest thing to agree to. Like that, rather than the laborious day we'd planned, we now had nothing but stretches of unscheduled time. The river and I would have a second chance.

This time, I descended alone. I brought a chair and a book. I wore sandals and shorts, and a loose top over a sports bra. The others planned to follow when they were ready. What might happen now that, finally, I was here alone?

Once again, I staggered into the shallows. Occasionally, I found a slightly less uncomfortable collection of stones and stopped, until my feet hurt again. Then I lurched on. I held my hands away from my body for balance, and to make it easier to catch myself if I fell – how an old person moves. The river winked in the sunlight, flashing down its staircase, sliding and broadening at the pool, and the silver trees stood like meditating druids while I stumbled on.

How could I hear what the water and I might do together? Whatever the trick, I clearly didn't know it. I wasn't any better at hearing it when I was alone.

I returned to shore. I left my feet bare and placed the chair several times before finding stable enough ground and something approximating shade. I opened my book. The water evaporated from my legs in tiny sparks. Perhaps I could be satisfied with this? My husband and son slithered down the path with a couple chairs and a backgammon board. My daughter and her boyfriend skidded behind them, determined to brave the water.

My daughter waded in, and I saw something of my recent self in her mincing steps and uncertainty. Her boyfriend, however, was a human otter who saw water as his playground. *I* was once a human otter. Now, my daughter's uncertain steps made me wonder what I'd done wrong that both of us moved so hesitantly?

The afternoon sun kept encroaching on my shade, determined to roast me. I shifted my chair again and again. My skin prickled with heat. I called to my daughter, "Honey, just get *in*. Stretch out on your belly and pull yourself around with your arms."

She waved a hand in my direction. "I know." She did not follow my instructions. Urgency gripped me, but I clamped down on offering further advice. She was a freshly minted twenty-four-year-old and perfectly capable of finding her own way.

I stood, and barely stopped myself from hollering, "Like this!"

My son and husband were deep into their backgammon game. I needed to demonstrate for my daughter the perfect way to get in among the bright stones. Then she could wander among them without foot pain, their glistening colors just inches from her nose. But no one paid me any attention.

Wait.

No one was paying attention.

A space opened in me, and I noticed *I* was the one who wanted to get in the river. Rather than tell my daughter what to do, I would do it myself.

I placed my book in the seat of the chair. Three steps brought me to the river. I bent and submerged my hands till they touched ground. The water reached just past my elbows. I shifted my weight toward the stones as I crouched, then stretched my legs behind. The cool water hit my warm thighs like a friendly *keisaku* stick. *Wake up!* I hit operatic notes, higher and higher octaves the further I submerged. Somehow this helped me with the transition, and finally, I was held in the palm of the river. I made my slow progress, a crayfish, bringing my stretched-out carapace along for the ride.

My daughter sat on a large stone at the center of the river. I recognized the look on her face: in love with water. She had found her way. Of course she had: I'd stopped watching her.

I pulled myself along with ease, and I could relish the glistening brick, fawn, and cerulean stones now that they weren't a source of foot pain. I sketched slow, small circuits along the riverbed, looking in front of my nose until I realized I could lift my head and look around.

I eyed the swimming hole and the large rocks on its far edge. Earlier, leaning over the fence, Garth and I had noticed signs that the water had been higher in the springtime, probably over the tops of these rocks. Now, a portion of it was dry just a couple feet above the water.

The undercurrent that ran through the swimming hole moved strong and steady. It was no more than forty feet across in total. No matter how out of shape I was, surely I had the strength to get myself there.

"I'm going across!" I announced and turned toward deep water.

My body remembered how to propel itself, and though its muscles were no longer practiced in these movements, and the heart and lungs were weaker than the last time I'd swum, still, I moved. The stony river floor fell away abruptly, and I was in the pool. Several feet more and the pale green current slipped and swirled around me. The temperature cooled the closer I paddled toward the center.

A strand of current pulled at me single-mindedly as I entered the strongest flow. I struggled to stay on course. I remembered long-ago instructions on how to extract oneself from a riptide, so I allowed the current to move me off course and swam on a diagonal instead. My breath came fast, and my heart thumped. Then, I was on the other side of the current and able to angle myself toward the stone.

The steep rock face nearest me was still underwater, but the river was so clear I could easily see a foothold. I grabbed a knob at the top of the rock, placed my foot and, riding the momentum from my sprint across, pulled myself up.

Water poured off my skin and clothes. The rock was a dark, charcoal gray, covered with bumps and divots. A shallow, elongated pool had formed on its surface. None of the dry spots offered an inviting place to sit, but finally I settled myself at one end where the bumps were slightly flatter. My shirt and shorts clung to my skin, and my chest heaved.

When I could breathe again, I raised my arms and crowed, "Woo-whoo!" Everyone looked up, grinned at my success, then turned back to their various activities. The opposite shore felt far away.

In the time since I'd first gone in the water, the sun had moved a slow meandering arc downriver. Where once it had shone on my chair, now the whole bank was in shade. Here, with the charred forest at my back, the sun remained, dappling my skin from behind the imperfect trees.

The top of the rock was longer than it was wide, like a dining room table with two leaves in. I sat at one end; the long pool stretched away from me. On its surface, water striders moved in their usual *skim-rest-skim-rest* manner. Though their bodies were almost invisible in the stippled light, I tracked them easily by the circle of shadow where each head-of-a-pin foot touched the water.

At the far end of the pool, a spider had built its web between two edges, the lower curve less than an inch above the pool's surface. Three water striders skimmed close to me. A fourth floated perilously close to the web. I stared, willing it to skim. It didn't. Maybe it had already encountered the spider and was dying or dead. This possibility gripped me. Two of the other striders seemed directionless in their journeys, but the third sculled a dogged path toward the strider by the web. Not usually one to anthropomorphize insects, tension clutched at my heart.

Over time, the stone and I slid into full sun. My skin tightened as it dried. The voices of my family were indistinct, little more than part of the backdrop of the singing river and the swishing trees. The sun warmed me to my bones. Further down the river, more rapids, followed by more stretches of calm, flashed and winked from reflected sunlight. Ashy trees rose behind me while on the opposite bank others climbed the hillside glowing green.

I remained in reverie until the suspense about the strider's plight loosened. When I glanced again at the pool, the fourth strider was moving! It skimmed alongside its rescuer, fleeing the spiderweb. I'd looked away and they had carried on; the rescue mission succeeded without any attention from me.

My muscles ached from all the effort. The lumpy stone pushed its knobs into my butt. I eyed my foothold. Given its angle, it wouldn't be especially useful getting back into the river. My re-immersion was likely to be ungraceful.

It was time. I plopped into the river and once again paddled through the water, through its gentle currents at the edge, then the swifter chill at the center, and finally to the opposite shore. I wasn't as strong as when I'd crossed in the other direction, but my body still had the strength and stamina I needed.

The others were ready to head back to the campsite, and we gathered our things. My thighs trembled on the steep incline.

The unhurried evening unfurled. We lit the camp stove and boiled water for dinner, and again for dishwashing. The boyfriend built a fire. My daughter whittled branches for marshmallow skewers. A few mosquitoes found us but were easily waved away. We settled in for an evening around the campfire, planning to remain until it was the only light in the gathering darkness.

I paid a last visit to the pit toilet, said good night to my family, then went to the tent. Its entrance opened toward the fire. I turned over my boots to keep the dew out. The ripping sound of the tent zipper evoked summers from my childhood, other fires and other rivers.

The inside window faced the water. I slipped loose pajama bottoms over my underpants. The night was still warm, but I liked having weight on me when I slept. I slid into the unzipped sleeping bag and pulled the top across me. No, too warm. Maybe if I slid my feet and lower legs out and kept the bag across just my thighs and belly... It was an improvement to be partially exposed. My thighs radiated heat. As close to the new moon as it was, even with my eyes open, the inside of the tent was pitch black.

Low voices and the crackle from the campfire sounded as if they were right beside me. No one could see me, though, so I folded back the sleeping bag and lifted my hips to slide off my pajama bottoms.

The cool air sparkled on my legs, its touch lighter than that of the river, as if it spoke to the spaces between my cells. My legs felt an irresistible desire to stretch toward the sky and I surrendered. They floated up, my feet less than a yard from the ceiling. My eyes stayed open, a strangely off-balancing sensation since I couldn't see a thing. My legs drew my attention again, the feel of them. Moments before, the barriers of skin and muscle felt themselves to be distinct from the atmosphere. Now, like a wildfire choosing to go this way and not that, these barriers slowly dissolved into the air.

Thoughts lifted from my mind as easily as my legs deciding to float: *I am the air; the air and I are one thing.*

My thoughts wanted to name what was happening, but the experience was purely physical. If I wanted to, I was sure I could follow the air out among the trees, up into the canopy, and spread into the sky.

I longed to rest in the hammock of this feeling. If only I could keep my thoughts at bay. Without them, I might linger in the space where the atmosphere and I entwined.

My mind could only still itself for so long, though, and it tumbled into, *Wow. This is amazing.* It couldn't stop itself from reaching for language, and before long, the skin of my legs divided me from the cooling air.

When my eighteen-year-old niece died from cancer, a stillness overtook me. From this fissure of calm, I effortlessly understood what was essential and what was not. There might be a perfectly logical, scientific explanation for why my legs became air: an altered state having to do with tired muscles, and cool air on warm skin, open eyes and pure darkness, all converging in one explicable "I am air" moment.

I prefer to think the river, the air, and the death of the forest created this familiar *bardo* for me, just as my niece's death had. The in-between state of the *bardo* emerges from profound loss. Out of this loss arises a chance to transcend our usual burdened way of being and to see truly—for a time. In the space created by the forest's death, I tasted my most essential self.

Gentle murmurs drifted from the campfire. I held my legs aloft a few more moments, then pulled them into the puffy sleeping bag. Beyond the tent, the river continued its journey over and around trees and stones, a journey that sounded like nothing so much as the wind. Or was it the wind that sounded like the river?

October Twilight

John Grey

Squirrels pause for apples
rolled half-down a hill.
At the edge of the forest,
nibbling deer fold up
into their own stillness.
Setting sun gilds half-naked trees,
the shivering pond.

Sounds have given way
to soft-shoe contact
of light and bough,
chill and stillness,
sky fresh-whelped of goose and songbird,
its breadth, a taciturn fading blue.

Crossing over into twilight,
the silent crowd
of falling leaves
bears no dissension
in their letting go.

The Eyes That See

Tammy Higgins

Cedar Waxwings in the Hospital's Playground

LindaAnn LoSchiavo

My youngest sister's dying first. That's not
How it's supposed to be—thoughts I push hard,
Harder, the small soprano in the swing
Flying to greet the blue with her high C.

She has her mother's eyes and begs for more
With promises she *will hold on!*—a good girl
Who's never-never-bound. Soon she won't fit
In this contraption, chubby legs too close
Already to the frame. I've just explained:
Some things grow fast like cedars—massing thick
Enough to matter, so strong they repel
Most other forces. High above us now
Cedars shield us from wind, block the cold rooms
Where promise grows, exposing flesh closer
To bones, a chest without hope, a matter
Of time. Trees near this playground stir, newborn.

Swift cedar waxwings bring their young treats, greet
A vast horizon, optimistic might,
As I try pushing so much weight away.

A girl on a swing, returns to me, again, again,
Protected, safe, and saved. Hold on, my love. Hold on!

About Face

Sylvia Sensiper

"But you would recognize *me*, wouldn't you?" I ask Joe a little anxiously.

"If there was a group of women that were similar in height and body shape and you were wearing something that you wouldn't usually wear and didn't have on your glasses," he says, "I'm not really sure."

It's a bit disconcerting that my partner of thirty-some-odd years isn't certain he would be able to find me in a crowded restaurant or, perhaps, even pick me out of a police line-up. I know he has accomplished the former many times in the past, but apparently his success relies on a great deal of context such as knowing what I'm wearing or recognizing my voice and gestures, and the latter, well, so far that hasn't been necessary.

My husband recently discovered he has face blindness or to use the more melodious scientific name, prosopagnosia. He has always had difficulty with remembering names, but the research he read on facial recognition provided a couple of aha! moments. It's not the process of getting people's names right that causes him problems, it's their faces he doesn't quite remember.

"When I switched from thinking about it as remembering and thought about it as recognizing," Joe says," I realized that what I'm unsure of is whether I've actually seen the face before. Most people say, 'oh, I recognize this face, but I just don't know the name.' I just don't recognize the face."

This self-diagnosis, I think, gives me the license to pester him with questions and test him on other visual parameters.

What about Andrew, I ask, referring to our grown son, could you pick him out of a crowd? Andrew lives in Colorado, and we talk by phone regularly and also FaceTime and Zoom. We visit in person at least two or three times a year.

"It might depend on how recently I'd seen him," Joe responds and I'm sure the expression on my face is a little incredulous.

"I think I would," he continues," but it's a tricky question. I want to say yes, but I always see him in a specific context. If he was sitting with a bunch of other people that kind of vaguely looked like him, in a place I didn't expect to see him, say, for example, a café where I had gone for fries, would I recognize him without hearing his voice? I don't know."

Joe and I met one spring very long ago when I gave a talk at a conference in Los Angeles for the Society for the Anthropology of Consciousness, a subunit of the American Association of the same discipline. The talks that day were on a range of topics that anthropologists commonly explore -- shamans, trance and spirit healers -- but that weekend many of the presentations veered into the personal with an uneasy focus on the strange experiences some of the researchers had during their fieldwork. My talk was more theoretical, and when Joe approached me afterwards to tell me we had a mutual friend in common, a fellow graduate student whom I had met earlier that year, we felt a common bond. That night, as some people took off into the hills to experiment with mushrooms (and yes, it was that kind of conference), and the rest of us took to dancing, Joe stood next to me in the circle and pointed out two older people moving together. "That's us in twenty years," he said, and the tone was so ambiguous that it was unclear whether he was alluding to their status as professors and our future careers, or that they were a couple.

After the conference, Joe and I did start seeing each other, a phrase that seems apt in defining our early relationship, and how I described it to friends. "I'm seeing someone," I would say, although there is some disagreement among recent online comments I've found as to whether 'seeing someone' denotes a category that is more serious than dating or if the metaphor infers there is very little commitment to the relationship. What the expression implies in my mind is certainly less than "love is blind," but also more than going out. You definitely aren't overlooking any personality peculiarities, but you do see something very special about that person that maybe isn't so apparent to others. Joe and I talked for hours on the phone, sent letters back and forth until he showed me how to use an early form of email, and drove up and down the California coast to visit our respective homes, once camping at the halfway point in Pismo Beach among an orange haze of monarch butterflies migrating south.

The expression 'seeing someone' seemed to fit the nature of our romantic interest at that point, but it is also a funny phrase to use now because I'm not actually sure, that had we bumped into each other out of context the week following the conference, say, walking down the street near the University of Santa Cruz where Joe had started graduate school the prior fall, would he have recognized me as the woman he had just met and spent time with?

When I ask him this question, he shrugs his shoulders and tries to explain again.

"I see all the parts and I know it is a face. But it's not *someone's* face. If a face for you is something that's recognizable as a person, then I don't see that kind of coherence. I guess that's the easiest way to say it."

Joe did become a professor once he finished his PhD, and now, after a couple more questions from me, he suggests I read the research exploring the various facets of face recognition. This is an understandable reaction and also classic Joe. If you express an interest in a topic, he has usually read something about it and whether you are one of his graduate students, a family member, a friend or just someone he recently met, he has a couple of papers and probably a book chapter he would like to share.

Joe makes a note in his phone to put the material in our shared Dropbox and then tells me with a smile, "It's a good thing I don't have Capgras syndrome."

After taking a look at the chapter he sends me about this neurological dilemma, a syndrome named after a French psychiatrist of the same name, I whole-heartedly agree. People with Capgras, whether due to an injury or psychological disorder, often come to regard those very close to them, parents, siblings, a spouse or a child, as imposters. The neurologist V.S. Ramachandran has hypothesized that people with this condition recognize faces just fine, but there is a disconnect between their temporal cortex, the part of the brain that carries out that function, and the limbic system, the part of the brain associated with emotions.

Ramachandran worked with a client named Arthur for over a year, a young man whose parents had begged the doctor for help. When Arthur saw his mom and dad and didn't experience the warm and loving feelings he associated with their presence, he made the plausible interpretation that they were not who they said they were and explained it this way. "That man looks identical to my father, but he really isn't my father. That woman who claims to be my mother? She's lying. She looks just like my mom, but it isn't her."[1]

Joe tells me that sometimes sufferers think their loved ones are clones or even aliens and after googling other research, I tell him about a really extreme case I read about. "There

---

[1] Ramachandran, V.S. and Blakeslee, Sandra. (1998). *Phantoms in the Brain: Probing the Mysteries of the Human Mind*

was one situation," I tell him, "where the guy thought his dad was a robot so he decapitated him so he could look for the batteries in his head."[2]

I also look at the research on super recognizers, people who can remember every face they've ever seen, even if they just catch a glimpse from the side as the face turns away or they see that person only for a moment. Super recognizers remember the faces of people they sit next to on a bus, pass by in a crowd walking down a busy city street or interact with for just a brief time while they purchase some fast food. They are also able to remember and identify people after many years because they can adjust for aging or a change in appearance.[3]

Although this might seem to be an enchanting 'super power,' people who have this ability realize that others may find it somewhat creepy. To avoid awkward social interactions, they usually refrain from using their magnified perception in ordinary circumstances.[4]

"Just think about it," Joe says, as we are cleaning up after dinner and having what has now become an on-going conversation. "What if you were introduced at a party and the person said, 'Nice to meet you but we've met before, five years ago when I served you tandoori at that Indian restaurant in Sacramento on 21st Street near N.' It would seem pretty odd."

Joe also reports to have found something similar, although on the reverse side of the spectrum.

"One time I was at a conference, and I was approached by this guy who asked me if I remembered him. When I honestly answered 'no', I realized that was the wrong thing to say because he looked so crestfallen. Ever since that time, I *never* say, 'no'.

Whether Joe would have remembered me out of context when we first started seeing each other is an unknown but what Joe *did* see was something other than what those close to me at the time perceived. To my family and my then-circle of friends, my life was a mess, although I preferred the use of the more generous phrase 'in transition.' I had recently left behind a failed marriage, filed for divorce, and was applying for a PhD program. I had also just bought a run-down fixer-upper in South Central LA that I was in the process of renovating. The roof had already been ripped off and replaced, the foundation shored up and the weekend Joe came into the picture (note the visual metaphor), the house was in the midst of another grand repair; the entire back wall was gone and covered over with a sheet of plastic.

"Are you serious about this young man?" my father asked, pulling me aside when I brought Joe to dinner at my parents' house a few months after the conference.

I nodded my head and thought to myself, why else did I invite him to meet you? Yet I knew the reasons my father felt the need for an interrogation.

Joe was rail thin, with long curly hair that he wore pulled back in a ponytail and although he didn't come barefoot to dinner, he did wear sandals. More worrisome to my dad, was that Joe was clearly younger than me, with a boyish face that would put him on the receiving end of the question 'what's the topic of your dissertation?' for many years after he had already become a successful academic and had many publications to his name.

My relationship with Joe added yet another element of concern to those close to me, my fractured existence, something that many in my circle just could not understand. Friends

---

[2] Further research has indicated that Capgras syndrome also involves brain damage to the right frontal lobe. https://www.washingtonpost.com/national/health-science/this-strange-syndrome-causes-people-to-think-their-loved-ones-have-been-replaced-by-identical-impostors/2018/04/06/0091f168-1be6-11e8-9de1-147dd2df3829_story.html

[3] Pearl, Sharrona. (September 2019). A super useless super hero: The positive framing of super recognition, *Semiotic Review 7*.

[4] Super recognizers are in high demand in security jobs where their ability to recognize faces often exceeds that of computers. They have been hired by the London Metropolitan Police and Scotland Yard, who reportedly has developed an elite squad (*The Guardian*, November 2016).

coming to visit me in South Central would get off Highway 80 at Western Avenue, proceed through the city streets marked with boarded up stores or those framed with bars, arrive at my house, see the disarray, and then usually react with alarm at what appeared to be a life in decline. 'It looks like you are living on the edge," I remember one friend commenting. But Joe saw something different. "I liked the idea that you were camped out in your own home, among all that drywall dust," he told me. "I could tell that wasn't who you were."

One could say that Joe and I met in an atmosphere of great openness and potential, but what we also had was context. We were both steeped in the concepts of anthropology, had started graduate programs at similar moments, and from our discussion following my presentation at the conference had determined we were kindred spirits.

"I depend on context a ton, you know," Joe says, articulating what many prosopagnosiacs assert. "If I'm teaching a graduate course this is where the graduate students are. At the beginning of a class, they may appear as faces that don't look distinct and more like collections of stuff. But over time, I get to know their work, I read their writings and see their websites. It's like the layers build up and they begin to hold together as a distinct person."

Joe is a popular professor so he must be doing something right with navigating context but the area of his life where he finds his face blindness to be the biggest liability is when he teaches undergraduate classes.

"I would love to be able to look at a room of 50 people or even 15 people and say, Jim, what do you think about this? If a student completes a really good assignment I would love to ask them a question, but I hate saying a name and then looking around and hoping. I'd like to be able to call on them and engage them."

Yet Joe's ineptitude to connect names with faces seems to have cultivated some implicit skills that are valuable in more personal interactions. "I think there's some kind of presence that comes with my inability to recognize faces. When I meet with a student, I am really listening to what they are saying right now, right in the moment. This happens even with people that I know really well. I don't really bring their past with me because it's just not there. I don't forget their history, but it doesn't intrude."

Joe has never been tested but the increased understanding of super-recognizers has helped neurologists to rethink face recognition as a capability that lies on a spectrum. They estimate prosopagnosia affects 2-2.5 percent of the population and another 10 percent have less than average proficiency at recognizing faces. Oliver Sacks, the well-known neurologist, not only wrote about his face blindness, but acknowledged that his prosopagnosia also affected his ability to identify places, and he often needed assistance to arrive at a planned destination. [5]

Joe also seems to have other sorts of absent-minded professor-type behaviors that may or may not be associated with his inability to recognize faces. He rarely notices if I get my hair cut or if I change the layout of the garden, and he has told me quite adamantly that he would not be able to determine which black couch was ours if it was placed alongside four others (It's actually brown). But there are so many lovely qualities that he attributes to his prosopagnosia that I think there's a trade-off. It's a wonderful thing to have a spouse who listens carefully and who has a real heartfelt openness to change. It is also reassuring to know that if I find myself covered in drywall dust again, whether real or metaphoric, my partner will know for sure that isn't who I really am.

Yet as someone who knows people by their faces and feels this is a necessary ability to successfully navigate the world, I still feel a bit of concern. Joe's compensation practices appear seamless, but our conversations have called to mind a few times when I've seen him acting a little shy in certain social situations and wondered what was at the root of that kind

---

[5] Sacks, Oliver. (2010). Face-blind: Why are some of us terrible at recognizing faces? *The New Yorker*.

of hesitation. I now assume those were moments when he was collecting information and listening with particular care to a person's voice and words to determine whether he had met them before.

The next time I talk with Andrew, I bring up the topic with him. "Dad thinks he has face blindness," I say, but Andrew just laughs. He knows his father as a very successful and sociable, if somewhat quirky, professor with a great propensity for theories, syndromes and research. Andrew has been on the receiving end of many books and articles himself in his twenty-nine years.

"Don't worry, mom," he tells me over Zoom. "If you ever go missing, we'll have someone else describe you to the detectives."

When I tell Joe about this conversation, he just smiles. "I will tell them you are small," he says.

Why Do We Always Get Lost?

Buff Whitman-Bradley

I take out the trash every afternoon
And bring it back in at night
You might think that's odd behavior for the king of France

There are bicycles scattered in everything I have forgotten
I have used all the maps to start campfires
The stars tonight are so loud I cannot sleep

When I drive my car I forget about old movies
It is difficult to concentrate while skidding on an iceberg
Why do we always get lost?

Pastel Pastiche

Andrew Graber

The Artist

Joel Robbins

A skilled, sun-tinted watercolor,
No flowers, just rock and ocean,
With splashed here and there a pier,
A fishing hut, crab boxes, a boat.
Her, long passed out of this world,
Somehow, still looking through the frame.
Her breath living in that pigment, paper,
the view she painted so carefully for us.

Beauty Is Pain

Becca Bullen

"There's nothing wrong with you, you're beautiful."

I was 17 years old when the pain started. It was immediate and crippling and confusing. I ate soup and smiled big and hoped the fourth dose of Advil today would do the trick. The pain was in my mouth, it began at my jaw bone and radiated across my face. I dismissed it every opportunity I could, telling myself it wasn't that big of a deal. Ignoring the fact that I woke up every night from extreme discomfort and was consuming more ibuprofen than I was solid food.

I've always found it so odd how people equate an outside appearance with the internal reality. Knowing full well that they personally, probably, have not always presented themselves with the kind of honesty to strangers that they now expect from me. All my life I have run from this idea: that to express my emotions is to be weak and that toughness and grit are more important than honesty. I was a "rub some dirt on it" kind of kid, not because it didn't hurt, but because I didn't want to be the kind of girl who said it did.

I remember sitting in the doctor's office, with the stark white walls and stiff leather chairs that groaned as you sat. The same office I sat in weeks prior before a routine surgery on my mouth. I remember the fountain that sat in the corner and the instrumental music playing throughout the waiting room, the faint smell of disinfectant clashing with the comforting atmosphere they were trying to create. It was beautiful, there was nothing wrong with it. I sat in the chair, so uncomfortable and out of place. I felt like I was taking up someone's time, like I was being impolite and inconvenient to the busy schedule of these strangers.

He walked into the office with a kind smile and shook my hand. He told me it was good to see me again. His smile turned into a puzzled smirk when I told him the pain I experienced. I told him about the soup and the Advil and I did so with my hair curled, my legs crossed, and my nails manicured.

As I detailed my pain to this surgeon he clung to the theory that I should have recovered by now, that my pain tolerance was low and that I was fine. Not just fine, beautiful. How could there be something wrong with me if I looked so beautiful? How could I have pain in my mouth when my face looked so perfect?

"There's nothing wrong with you, you're beautiful."

As if both couldn't be true. I realize that as a medical professional he reasoned that if there had been something wrong underneath, there would be evidence of this on the surface. But my face wasn't swollen, I didn't show up into the office in pjs with tears in my eyes. Should I be flattered? I told my Mom that I thought I might be going crazy. That if the pain I was feeling was truly in my head, then there must be something wrong with my head.

A few weeks later my Mom drove me back to that office. I was led to the back room where I performed my routine of explaining that it hurt to eat; that it hurt all the time.

Through clouds of clear frustration my doctor said that he was willing to make a deal. He said he would do me the generous favor of putting me under and slicing open my face just to show me how healthy I am. Just to show me how crazy I am. Just to show me how beautiful I am.

According to a study conducted by *Health Services Research,* one in five women reported gender-discrimination when going to the doctor or health clinic. Compared with male patients, women who present with the same condition may not receive the same evidence-based care. Oftentimes, women may get different treatment, leading to poorer outcomes.

As I awoke from the haze of drugs, I heard that same serene music. I slowly blinked my eyes open and began to vaguely remember where I was, and why I was here. The nurses and assistants in the room gave me soft smiles and filled the room with silence. They looked at me with such pitiful eyes and I knew it was my craziness or my drugs or my low pain tolerance that made them so empathetic. My face hurt, but this time I could feel the stitches in my mouth as evidence of the damage done.

It wasn't until my mom was driving me home for recovery that she told me I was right. She told me that when he opened me up he found my face beaten and shattered and devastated underneath all my beauty. The part of my face that had been hurting so much was my jaw bone. I had developed something called osteomyelitis, an infectious disease which had caused small pieces of my jaw bone to break off. The doctor pulled out all the diseased pieces and stitched me back together. I felt such devastating relief at the idea that there was proof of my pain, that I really wasn't the girl with the low pain tolerance who needed to grow some tough skin.

On the next visit to the beautiful office, I awaited my apology from the doctor who called me beautiful. I thought he would tell me he was sorry for not believing me. Instead, he told me I was a tough cookie.

"If you had cried," he said, "then I would've believed you. You were just so stoic and you didn't look sick."

If I had cried, he would've believed me.

Hysteria is derived from the Greek word for womb. Since the late fifth-early fourth centuries BC, when women expressed their emotions they have been deemed hysterical. In Ancient Greece, this hysteria is what prohibited a woman from having basic rights, from holding political office, and from receiving an education. According to Greek legend, a woman's uterus could move, and when it did it would make its way up to the woman's head and this is what caused her hysteria. This is the theory of the wandering womb, a condition only women experienced that explained away all of their inconvenient feelings. Women diagnosed with this condition would go to great lengths to get their uterus to move back down, sometimes resorting to outright strange and painful treatments. This was the primary reason women weren't accepted in this society; it would be absolutely ludicrous to allow women to hold important positions within a society when they have no control over their behaviors or emotions.

"There's nothing wrong with you, you're beautiful."

If the doctor had found the diseased bone sooner, I wouldn't have needed such intense treatment. After realizing my face wasn't going to heal as efficiently as they had hoped, I was sent to another doctor who placed a PICC line in my arm for intravenous treatment. Every day I did my homework while receiving my treatment in the living room, the home-health nurse would clean my line and then I would lie on the kitchen counter while my Mom washed my hair, knowing I couldn't do it by myself. I wasn't allowed to lift anything heavy, or get my heart rate up. My athletic body turned slim and my independence disappeared.

I cried every night when the pain in my face was too unbearable to fall asleep. I cried when I couldn't eat my favorite foods because it hurt too bad. I cried when I struggled to dress myself in the early mornings before school. I cried because I told him where it hurt and he convinced me it didn't. I cried because I was beautiful. But most of all I cried because I believed if I had only done it sooner, if I had shed a tear in his beautiful office maybe he would've believed me. Maybe he thought I had a wandering womb. Maybe it was my fault I didn't look sick enough.

If I had cried, he would've believed me.

Perhaps if I had come into the office looking like a mess. If I had sobbed into his big arms and shrieked with anguish as I recounted my daily agony. Maybe if my hair was unbrushed and my nail polish was chipped he'd see that I really was suffering. Or maybe he could've believed the words that escaped my lips rather than the length of my eyelashes or the silver chains hanging around my neck.

Women are seven times more likely than men to be misdiagnosed and discharged in the middle of having a heart attack. This is because the medical concepts of most diseases are based on an understanding of male physiology, and women altogether have different symptoms than men when having a heart attack. When the doctor told me the pain in my face was the result of low pain tolerance I immediately became a statistic; I wonder if I was a man if he would have told me I was too sensitive. I wonder if a man has ever been told he was too handsome to be in pain.

Despite changes throughout female representation in medicine, stereotypes and underrepresentation of women in the medical community persist. Females are more often told when presenting a medical concern that their complaints are the result of too much stress, depression, anxiety, or hormonal cycles. Women oftentimes choose to be more passive and constrained when expressing their pain or complaints so as not to overreact and harm their credibility with the medical professional. Once credibility is destroyed, a woman is often subject to a false psychogenic diagnosis rather than an accurate medical diagnosis. In other words, we fulfill the prophecy of the Greeks and tell our women they have a case of the wandering womb. How far we have come, and how far we have left to go.

Beautiful bodies can still carry ugly pain. For so long I blamed myself for being too polite, for being too stoic, for being too put together. I figured I must've miscommunicated my pain and sabotaged my own healing because of my inability to correctly express my impolite emotions. It was not until much later that I realized my voice was one of many women who had been misheard, not who had misspoken. The way I looked and the number of tears that left my eyes should not have been trusted over my word and my diagnosis should not have been delayed because of a doctor's fascination with my pain tolerance. I recovered from my surgeries and finished my last round of treatment, but part of me was forever changed. I couldn't stop thinking about the other women whose wombs wandered too far; I couldn't stop thinking about the beautiful, hysterical, sensitive patients who asked their doctors to see their pain for what it is.

There's nothing wrong with you. You're beautiful.

The Great Highway

Kurt Cline

Cold & clear   sky cerulean
Awakening a dream she could sink in
A little shadow-play
On sheets of white—

An apparition in flight!

A barista becomes
A nymph carrying
A coffee-urn—

On whose orders precisely?

Doesn't matter now
but later   let my ashes
There be scattered

Where the riptide
Gets ripped
Every evening

Raven on the red-
Light lamppost
Arching over
The Great Highway

Where morning rocks
And it seems like I'm okay.

Note: The Great Highway, built in 1929, forms the western edge of San Francisco and runs for three miles along Ocean Beach, where Cline's ashes were scattered.

Chasing a High, Lawrence, Kansas

James P. Cooper

Sun Ra

Kurt Cline

Sun Ra
>   rakes across the late sky
>   seagull feathers
>   strewn in the sand

Jet plane
>   streaking across the horizon
>   raven on the lamppost
>   arching over the Great Highway

Songbirds make
>   sixteenth-notes on phone lines—
>   fancy arpeggios before flying away
>   into the dark of stars smudges in the mist

As the future
>   has to be anyway following soul-waves
>   wherever they go   the earth speaks
>   the sea listens

The universe
>   (not entirely invisible
>   teaches my eyes to see things
>   only a dream will tell.

Molting

Debra Solomon Baker

This summer's synchronous arrival of cicada broods XIII and XIX has brought some entomologists to the edge of ejaculation. After all, in this nutty 24th year of the third millennium, one where we've already been granted an extra (leap) day to garden, and the chance to snap 8000 selfies in solar eclipse specs, now we have this? A double emergence of adjacent cicada gangs?

Scientists claim that interbreeding is unlikely, but, you know, as a dating woman with degrees in the humanities, I think that's hogwash. I mean, there's not one Brood XIII guy who's gonna swipe right on a Brood XIX'er babe, put on his best avocado print button-down, and say, "Hey sweetie, head on over to this side of the bar and lemme buy you a Tito's and tonic?"

I remember the last time that Midwesterners got all agog about cicadas. For me, it had been a year of telling thirteen-year-old Jacob to pull up his mask, and of spraying the classroom desks with that covid-be-damned yellow liquid that would leak onto my fingers every hour. "Stand back," I would tell my middle schoolers, "Here come your chemicals. Don't say I never gave you anything." I gave you plenty of underrated teacher jokes.

I wore an "I Survived the 2020-2021 School Year" crown in the farewell parade for our students, and then drove from Saint Louis to Bloomington to visit a man I'd been dating.

This professor and I had outsmarted Covid in a whirlwind romance filled with umpteen nose swabs, 3 hour and 46 minute commutes, and plenty of fru-fru cocktails with mezcal and pink peppercorns. We had hiked through forests, and skewered kabobs, and dreamed of meeting at the Ryman Auditorium to hear Patty Griffin strum her guitar. We had flicked off 2020 with sushi in front of a fireplace on New Year's Eve.

And now, we were there in Indiana among the beady-eyed critters with the badass band name, Brood X. These "periodical cicadas" garnered so much attention that Amazon carried "Let Me Sing You the Song of my People: Cicada Concert 2021" tee shirts for $17.99. Fourteen reviewers gave the product five stars. These were desperate times.

On our stroll through campus, I flicked one little guy off of my shoulder, screamed "oh-crap-he's-on-my-cheek," slapped my left ankle, and then we skipped around the dead ones who were soldered to the concrete.

These sidewalks transformed into Old Country Buffet. Crowds could elbow their way in, load up plates with as many little critters as could fit beside lumpy mashed potatoes, butter-slathered dinner rolls, and candied yams.

And after unbuttoning the skinny jeans, those brave ones could head back for round two of this all-you-can-eat cicada bonanza.

Yes, these babies were edible, but I did not partake. I did not air-fry tempura cicada with sriracha aioli, and I am certainly not a bug enthusiast. Until recently, I had known two facts about the whole insect kingdom: the little guys have no backbone, and they do not experience pain.

I was 52 years old then, and my DSB vs. LJB documents were back home, crammed into a blue folder marked with a Sharpie, "How to Get A Divorce." Inside, there was a reminder that I had scribbled during a session with my therapist: "be gentle...talk to yourself the way that you talk to your students..." There was the Volvo VIN number, the Commerce Bank statement, something called Respondent's Counter-Petition for Dissolution of Marriage.

I stored the folder inside the drawer of a bedside table that I had wanted to list on Facebook Marketplace when I sold our home.

"I only need one," I'd told my used-to-be life partner.

"But the tables are a pair," he had replied. "You really should take both. They shouldn't be separated."

Shortly after he and I separated, our teenage children wrote a dating profile for me. *"Likes to read. Likes writing. Isn't social. Likes to stay home a lot."*

We call this later-in-life rupture a Gray Divorce. A Wrinkly-Knees Divorce. A Hot-Flashes Divorce. A WTF-are-Tinder-and-Bumble-I-Barely-Know-How-to-Answer-my-Phone Divorce.

And, yet, I had begun, right then, to swipe right.

Jeff: 6'1", active, undergraduate degree, drinks socially, smokes never, and has dogs. He's 47.

Nice eyes, Jeff, I type.

He says that he's scrolling Bumble and Facebook to "see what's happening in this crazy world." He says, "It's making everyone nuts honestly! Stir crazy is a real thing!"

Making everyone nuts. It's? The protests? The virus? The destruction of our planet? Humidity? The dwindling of the bee population?

"I'm a teacher," I type, and he responds, "MUCH MUCH MUCH respect and admiration for ALL teachers!"

Even the shitty ones, Jeff? Even the ones who sit at their desk, ignoring the chaos, solving crossword puzzles?

"Would you be open to a fwb honestly considering both of our situations?" he asks.

I use Google Translate.

"But we're not friends," I type.

"Would you consider yourself sexual," he types. "I like two of your photos in particular."

The one where I am holding an alpaca in a village in Ecuador? Or where my big sister and I are gripping gelato cones in Florence? Where I am sitting on a wall in a tank top and a boy shorts bikini, the one where my belly looks flat, my legs are firm, almost as if I've been giftwrapped with photoshop?

I ask him why he's getting divorced.

"Because she's a controlling verbally abusive narcissistic type A who isn't kind."

Oh.

"Also, her and I haven't had sex in YEARS."

She and I. She and I.

I type, "Oh." Then, "Were you having sex with other people?"

"I did have a friend at one point. I won't lie," he types.

"How long were you married to the verbally abusive narcissist who wouldn't have sex with you," I ask.

Later, Jeff Lastnameunknown will bumble-message that he broke off with his married "friend" because she was careless. Later, he will invite me to send him a special kind of photograph. He will add a smiley emoji.

Later, he will inquire, "Are you looking for serious or casual(ish)?"

Well, Sweetheart, I'm looking for ways to snap shut a 25-year marriage. And there ain't no shiva for stuff like this, no selection of overpriced wooden caskets in which to lay the deceased. I'm trying to scribble a eulogy for the marriage that once was beautiful, to honor those moments, to write condolence cards with x's and o's and little "I love you" messages to myself, like every single day.

I'm looking for stories, Jeff, stories to laugh away grief that suffocates me when I hear a Springsteen tune on Spotify, for how-to guides on dating when you have wrinkly knees, a sagging ass, and when there is a virus lurking on countertops, on Amazon packages, on doorknobs. I'm looking for my tallest mountain pose and for a collection of cleansing breaths, looking for ways to keep a pile of sourdough starter alive, to know the just-right amounts of flour and water and love that it needs, so that it doesn't later tell me that it feels broken and neglected, and weak. I am looking to season my fear with sprinkles of something more than xanax, looking for a symphony of self-love, and, maybe, Jeff, for someone who says, wow, you look gorgeous when you pile your hair atop your head like that, who whispers, I see you, Debra, yes, I see you.

Male cicadas arrive above ground first, paving the way for their lady-friends. After a protracted silent retreat down in their man-caves, they are there, ready to compete in this bug freeforall, in this full-on summertime orgy. Yes, these insects surpass even middle schoolers in their hormone-ocity. And then, sometimes, this fungus called Massospora creeps near them, and holy jesus, Mr. Masso brings those cicada boys down to their knees, rendering them genital-less and even more sex-manic than normal.

When that happens, well, park your toddlers in front of their screens. This shit gets crazy.

Cicadas do not need to wear thongs or pop 50 mg of Viagra one hour before springing into the hanky-panky. They do not need to use a wax strip on their upper lip, to light two candles for ambiance or to kick a mutt off of a lumpy queen-sized bed. They do not need to swipe left on dudes who post blurry mirror-selfies, who say, "After work you can find me at the gym.".

Cicadas copulate and then they die. And somewhere in there, the hardcore females lay 500 eggs.

One day, we are putting sixty bobby pins into our hair to get the curls just-right for all those photographs, drinking champagne from fancy flutes, dancing the hora, unwrapping the new waffle iron, and then, we are dividing up assets, and I'm messaging to see if he wants the wrought-iron lawn chairs for his one-bedroom apartment.

On the first Friday night after my husband moved out, I yanked up some carpet inside of my closet, transferred a few dresses from my closet into his, filled the top drawer of his dresser with my underwear and bras, put the sexiest ones on top just in case he came home one day and opened it expecting to see forgotten boxer shorts. Maybe he would see some lace, sink to the hardwood floor, cancel the appointment with the mediator. Joan Didion calls this magical thinking.

I dragged a rug up from the basement that night, and then dragged it back down. I found a checklist online that showed eight hundred things to ask a divorce attorney. I considered taking a bubble bath after reading some article claiming that you burn as many calories in a hot bath as you do while running, but it seemed like bullshit.

I set photographs of the kids and of my sister on the table next to his side of the bed. I leaned my Harvard diploma against the wall and listened to the dogs breathe. I approved of the outfit that our daughter planned to wear on her maybe-date with some boy named Isaac. It was a leopard-patterned crop top and I could see her belly button.

"You don't like it?" she asked.

"No, I do," I said. "You look so beautiful."

I watched Ellen Degeneres on Netflix, ate forty Honeymaid chocolate graham crackers, checked my phone dozens of times. He texted me that night, "maybe we can get dinner tomorrow, all four of us." The whole family.

"No," I said. "I've got plans." I did. I would buy a red shirt with a tie in the front and drink half a bottle of prosecco.

Days after sharing the "daddy's moving out" news with our two teenagers, I landed in Florida and drove to see the sunrise on Delray Beach. At the shore, there was a man, his arms held out high; his body was a cross. Hundreds of seagulls danced above him, beside him, and down below at his sandaled feet. It was a ceremony. The waves were their music and he, their canopy.

"Would you send me a photograph of this?" I asked some woman, a stranger standing nearby with a phone.

A line of pink brightened the horizon.

Later, she texted me, "Bird Man," along with a few photographs.

I typed back, crying, telling this stranger about the separation and about his phobia of birds, about how we could never go to the beach together because of the seagulls, how that was one of so many things that I wished we could have shared.

"So sorry to hear about ending your marriage," she answered. "Even when it's best, it is hard. Be sure to go to the beach again. I go nearly every day."

Cicada nymphs withstand huge falls. When only the size of a grain of rice, they drop from tree branches onto the ground, and there, they begin to dig. And, during the days and months and years spent burrowing, spent shedding their exoskeletons, the little guys suck nourishment from the roots that are resting nearby.

These roots whisper lullabies, cradling us when we are afraid of our darkness, of that which seems so terribly uncharted. They are bird men, they are friends who soothe like lines of poetry, they are the faith that, one day, that blue divorce folder will sit in a recycling bin, a mere relic of the dirt that once threatened to suffocate. These roots, they steady us, as we molt.

Carousel Ride

Joan Penn

Sitting astride a brightly-colored carved wooden horse,
eyes closed, hands gripping the reins, shouting *giddy-up*
as the carousel speeds up, imagination klieg-lit

with technicolor scene
featuring my seven-year-old-self
dressed like a cowgirl,

big-brimmed hat, kerchief knotted around neck,
chaps flapping against the horse's flanks,
dusty leather boots with spurs on them,

looking like an actor I'd seen in a Western,
galloping alongside of him at breakneck speed
across a CinemaScope-sized movie screen,

no fences to hem me in,
free from parental restrictions,
self-directed,

giving voice to the dialogue inside of me...

Sunrise over a Kansas Field

Izzy Lippincott

Where Dreams Take Place

Andrea Reynolds

Though I'm nearly 100 years old,
most of my dreams
take place in my childhood
flat. It doesn't matter
the premise.

Last night, I was 75
bickering with my skinny husband
over watering the lawn, but I
was in my 7-year-old bedroom.
Bright wallpaper with petals
shaped like teardrops spinning
pink and orange.

Tiny lime green tiles flew
off of the fireplace.
The hairline crack in the plaster
edged toward my sister's bed.
And I was yelling, *Stop
watering the grass.*

On Bilbo

Mark Lewandowski

Not the hobbit, Son of Belladonna and Bungo, but the cat, Son of Smokey and Unfixed Philanderer. We had never seen Unfixed Philanderer, but assumed Bilbo inherited his coloring. Over the top of his body spread a field of calico--a fine brown bordering on orange—while underneath glowed a brilliant, unblemished white. His mother was pure tortoise shell, a dark brown spiked with gold. The first four in the litter were quickly adopted out. Despite my mother's proclamation that one cat was enough, Bilbo, my sisters decided, would not be offered up. He was simply too cute and too cuddly, so when people came cat hunting to our house, Bilbo, conveniently, wasn't available. It's likely he was hidden in a closet.

No one wants him, my sisters cried. My mother sighed. Just a couple months old Bilbo had the uncanny ability to leap onto your pant leg and scale your body, right up to your shoulder, without even slightly grazing your skin with his claws. After his ascent he'd perch on your shoulder, really for as long as you could take it, occasionally dipping his cold little nose into your ear. Seeing Bilbo up there on her kids' shoulders made my mother crack a small smile. After the kitten climbed her, my mother relented, and Bilbo remained.

Maybe six months after her first litter, Smokey became pregnant again. (Why my parents didn't have her fixed I couldn't say.) Soon after she pushed out those seven little slimy puff balls, Smokey bailed. For days at a time. We looked down at that mewling mass and scolded their deadbeat mother. A number of the kittens had the same coloring as Bilbo, so we assumed Smokey had once again cavorted with Unfixed Philanderer.

Annie, my youngest sister, tried to feed the kittens milk, offering them slurps from a teaspoon. They wouldn't take it. While Smokey occasionally slithered back, we suspected these poor kittens were destined for a shoebox burial in the backyard.

Bilbo, however, would have none of that. One morning he sprinted inside with a squirrel in his mouth and bee-lined into the basement. By the time we got down there, he had dropped his kill in front of his brothers and sisters and they had tucked in, nibbling through hair and hide for openings just large enough to accommodate their pink snouts and darting tongues. It was pretty gross, all that slurping. Once satiated, they licked each other clean, wasting not one bloody bit.

Even without the consistent servings of mother's milk, the kittens lengthened and widened, and miraculously, all of them survived, even the runt we named "Frodo," on account of the resemblance to his older brother. Various friends and neighbors snatched up the first six quickly. We held back Frodo in hopes my mother wouldn't notice a third cat. Forget it, she said. Two cats are enough. So off went Frodo. Not too long after that, Smokey skedaddled for good. We remembered my mother's pronouncement and took it as permission to secure another cat. Forget it, our mother said. One cat is enough. Sometimes we just couldn't get our heads around Parent Logic.

So we made do with Bilbo, which was fine, since if you had to settle for just one cat, you couldn't ask for better. Unlike Smokey and the cats before her, Bilbo would not slink off to some hidey hole in the house. If he wasn't on a lap he sprawled on top of the television, often reaching down with a paw to chase a football or hockey puck on the screen. Even our mother remained charmed.

He would, however, disappear for hours at a time to hunt outside. Typically he went in and out through the sliding door separating the family room and back patio. Often, when he wanted back in, he launched himself at the screen and the glass door behind it, resulting in a loud **thunk** audible anywhere else in the house. He remained splayed against the screen, each contorted limb firmly affixed, like an overzealous beginner on a rock climbing wall. Not until we opened the door did he clumsily remove each claw from the quickly fraying screen and drop to the patio before sauntering in to use the litter box. More often than not he had been successful on his hunt. Squirrels, birds, chipmunks, mice, etc. ended up on our family room rug. This did not please our father.

One December night Bilbo, as usual, went out. It was already pretty cold in our little corner of Overland Park, Kansas. At least winter prey was rare, so if my father was home when Bilbo returned we wouldn't have to listen to him grumble and swear under his breath on sight of a rodent sucking in its last breaths on the rug.

Within an hour after Bilbo left the house the temperature plummeted. For the first time, he didn't return the next morning, or the one after that. Just a few days before Christmas the temperature dropped to -21. My father grumbled and swore under his breath while he worked the water pipes with a hair dryer. My sisters and I bundled up and spread out across the neighborhood calling Bilbo's name. We returned frozen and heartbroken.

A week passed, and then another. My father shook his head and told us he was sure Bilbo found a nice warm home somewhere. We nodded and did our best to believe him, hoping there was some sense to this Parent Logic.

And then one Sunday my father and I were watching football and **thunk**, there Bilbo was, velcroed to the screen. Astonished, we opened the door and pried him off. The poor thing looked half his fighting weight. Parts of his hide were matted with grime, other parts slippery with oil, and the tips of his ears were discolored. My sisters swept in and bundled him in a towel. Likely too wiped out to resist, Bilbo tolerated the bath they gave him, and soon fell asleep to their cooing and prodding.

"The oil on him," my father said, shaking his head. "He must've got up into a car's undercarriage to stay warm. I'll be damned."

Later that week, after hearing the story, the vet said Bilbo's survival was impossible, but there he was, already rebuilding his body mass. His ears were frostbitten, but he'd be fine. At the end of January, we found the blackened tips on the stairs. The rest of Bilbo was happily snoozing in a pile of blankets in my sisters' room. He didn't seem to miss those tips at all. Now he had rounded mouse ears. They looked perfectly natural, as if he'd been born that way. Then and there we announced he was the cutest cat ever. It wasn't the first time we had proclaimed this, but now we really, really meant it.

At a mall in downtown Kansas City, there was a wondrous store devoted to cats. One spring day the store hosted a cat party, so Annie crated up Bilbo, and my mother took them downtown. As it turned out, Hallmark, which is headquartered in Kansas City, had reps at the party, hoping to discover new talent. They looked at Bilbo and his rounded ears and flipped. We were sure they thought Bilbo the cutest cat ever, but were smart not to make too much of a fuss. There were other cats about; they didn't want to hurt their feelings, let alone alienate all their card-buying owners. One of the reps did, however, slip Annie a business card, and some weeks later Bilbo found himself again downtown, posing in front of red candles while a professional photographer clicked away. Hallmark cut Annie a nice check and promised Bilbo would one year appear in a calendar.

Neither his new gig as model, nor his near death experience kept Bilbo from prowling the neighborhood for critters and birds, even during the most inclement weather. He still wouldn't eat his catch. Sometimes we couldn't even figure how he killed these animals, since they rarely had a mark on them. Even though he no longer had siblings to feed, he continued to try to bring his victims into the house and drop them in front of us. When he couldn't sneak in his quarry he left it on the back porch.

By the mid-1980s, our father was becoming an avid birdwatcher. (He'd eventually become a certified Master Birdwatcher after identifying 500 species.) As the carcasses piled up, he grew more and more impatient with our beloved cat. (Even the dead chipmunks and squirrels made him angry, though some years later he'd buy a pellet gun and pick off the squirrels trying to raid the bird feeders.)

One spring day our father came into the house carrying a dead chickadee in a napkin and we knew Bilbo had drawn the last straw. A chickadee, my mother's favorite bird.

"That damn cat," our father shouted. "No more! One more dead animal and that cat is going to the Farm!"

We didn't really know what this Farm was. Some sort of glue factory, but for perfectly healthy cats instead of broken-down race horses? Whatever goodwill Bilbo had accumulated for saving a litter of kittens, or his miraculous resurrection, or his fifteen minutes of Hallmark fame had been exhausted. One more corpse and our dear Bilbo was history.

We stopped letting him out, no matter how much he cried and pawed at the door. But we couldn't stop my parents from letting him out, and they did, and more often than not we heard the familiar **thunk** against the door, and there was Bilbo on the screen with a still twitching cardinal clamped in his jaw. How many we chucked into the neighbors' yards I quickly lost count.

One evening my mother was working a late shift at the craft store. My sisters and I waited for my father to get home for supper. We were already nervous. Things were tense at his job, we knew, since we sometimes heard him talk to my mother in hushed whispers about it. Having to make us dinner wouldn't please him either. He was due any minute when Bilbo showed up at the back door. He hadn't launched himself at the screen—which was odd—but we were too relieved to see he wasn't carrying a dead chickadee to think much about it. As I slid open the door, he reached down and plucked up the dead squirrel hidden from view and zipped into the house. He stopped in front of the television and dropped it. As usual, there wasn't a mark on it. My sisters and I sat frozen. Bilbo licked his front paws before ambling off for a snack.

What do we do? What do we do?

I retrieved a snow shovel from the garage and my sister Mary toed the squirrel onto the blade. Out the back door I went. Sure enough, the neighbor on the right was mowing the lawn, and the one on the left was messing about with a bush. And forget the lady behind us; there she was staring out her kitchen window. She had gone full Gladys Kravitz after we fed her emaciated dog a steak.

Balancing the squirrel on the shovel I ran to the front house expecting my father to be turning into the driveway. My luck held, but for how long? There was the garbage can in front of the garage door. In went the squirrel. The can was empty except for a few inches of water at the bottom. I eventually found the lid and replaced it. A few minutes later my father pulled in. We sat waiting on the couch. Annie held Bilbo. He'd always had a loud purr. Now it really filled the room

"Hi, Dad," Mary shouted. "How was work?"

"Yeah, well," he grumbled, going straight into the kitchen.

Cabinet doors opened and closed. Then the refrigerator. A chair scrapped against the linoleum. After a minute or two, he walked back down the hallway towards the front door with the kitchen garbage.

Oh, shit.

"Weren't you supposed to take that out?" Mary asked.

He came back into the house. We braced ourselves.

"You'll never believe this," he said. "It's the damnedest thing. Somehow, someway, a squirrel got into the garbage can and drowned. And the lid was on!"

Was he serious?

"I think I put the lid on today," Annie said. "I guess I didn't notice it?"

"It's the damnedest thing," my dad said. He shook his head and went back to the kitchen to cook the spaghetti.

Parent Logic, we thought.

Still purring, Bilbo jumped off Annie's lap. For now, he had escaped the Farm. Oblivious to the close call, he rubbed up against each one of us, then sauntered over to the back door and pawed at the glass.

Luxembourg Gardens, Paris

Steven Pelcman

The sun tilts backwards
And an early moon grows larger
As the last narrow streams of light
Sprawl across a bed of flowers
And separates row by row!

A moth sits still, its wings
Clasped on white daisy petals,
And begins to spread out and thinly
Curl around a yellow heart as the sky
Shuts its eye at days end.

Have you ever noticed when a moth
No longer resists the wind or knows its way
in the dark, it becomes motionless
And turns inward losing more
Of itself as darkness appears.

White on white like a mother
To a child, it falls asleep
Amongst petals grown wild
Into the sweetest death
It could ever know.

Kansas Ziggurats

Izzy Lippincott

Japanese Beetle Trap

William Derge

They've made a flimsy green lace
of my pole bean leaves, that look
now like the lead frames of
stained-glass windows *sans* glass,
sans a reason to exist,
sans photosynthesis,
meaning, no flowers; no beans.

I lured them into entrapment with
a promise of sex, using the vice
squad's oldest trick, not by
laptop or cell phone,
but by pheromones. Male and female
flop into the yellowed sack,
a Noah's ark without a rainbow attached,
and one by one, like innocent plowboys
just off the bus, who stumble
into a brothel to ask
for a cup of kindness, they
suddenly don't want to leave, fallen
angels straight out of *Paradise Lost*.

In just a week, the den
of perdition fills up, Milton's
beehive in Hell, to tweak the
extended metaphor a dactyl more.
Still, the legions come, the oldest of
species to the oldest profession.

I don't quite know what to do
with a host of bugs in a bag,
most of whom, though weakened
with an excess of lust,
still manage to survive.

Don't ask me how
I manage to sleep at night.
I know the trade-off's uneven.
With a measure of regret,
I toss the beetles into the trash,
a thousand souls for what
won't amount on my plate
to more than a hill of...
Well, you know.

My Father's War

Wayne Glausser

For Wayne E. Glausser, Sr. (1917-1999)

My father did not serve in the military during World War II. He was 24 at the start of the war, healthy, big and strong (at 6'2" and 200 lbs., he had played football and worked in a steel mill), and patriotic. He had all of the qualities that people admire in members of the Greatest Generation—with the glaring exception that he did not make himself available for military service. Why didn't my father go off to war like the other men?

It's a question that has lingered in my mind since grade school. All of my friends' fathers had war stories; most of their living rooms featured photos of men in uniform looking heroic. In my own house today, there hangs a photo of my wife's father as a handsome lieutenant about to invade France. My father's younger brother enlisted and flew bombing missions as a navigator. One of his uncles was killed at Luzon in the Philippines near the end of the war. Why did my father stay home?

Many years after his death, I'm going on a modest quest to find out. I want to gather enough evidence to create the effect of communicating with my father about something we never talked about; to initiate, in other words, a sort of mind meld. I hope to complete my memory of the man whose name I share. And along the way, I commit myself, while surmising the risks involved, to a makeshift ethical evaluation of his decision.

Like my father, I came of age during a war with a draft. I provoked arguments every evening about the Vietnam War; we divided along predictable generational lines. As things turned out, my draft situation never rose to a crisis. My birthday (July 10th) came up as number 158 of the 365 slots chosen during the Selective Service lottery for 1971. During the year when I was exposed to the draft with a classification of I-A, the defense department did not draft past number 125. July 9th, the day before my birthday, drew the shortest stick of all—number 001. Had I been born just a few hours earlier back in 1951, that is to say, the Vietnam arguments between my father and me would have taken on much greater urgency. All these years later, I am trying my best to figure it out: what he might have advised me to do, and how he might have explained his own decision to sit out a much more popular war.

My father made his decision about the draft at a time when men were under intense pressure to serve in the military. Messages about patriotic duty permeated the culture. Among many other vehicles of persuasion, popular music linked military status with virility and romantic success. The WWII coupling of Venus with Mars must have been very difficult for a young man to withstand. Many songs during the war gave voice to women waiting faithfully for their soldier sweethearts. Any men *not* fighting were inherently unworthy. According to the 1943 song "They're Either Too Young or Too Old," for example, "what's good is in the army"; the draft board has left American women with the dregs. This song was popularized by the Jimmy Dorsey band, a band my father loved. Even before American entered the war at the end of 1941, one hit song sent out a clear message about draft classification and romantic desirability: "He's I-A in the Army and He's A-1 in My Heart." The singer draws parallels between the draft board's "physical" and the physical assets most prized by a woman. Her own sweetheart has "passed the toughest physical"; then she adds, more suggestively, "he ain't missin' nothing." Men who deviate from I-A classification implicitly come under suspicion as romantically defective. "He's I-A in the Army" is catchy and was recorded by two other bands my father loved, Les Brown's and Harry James's. He must have heard it often enough after he sought, and received, classifications that were not I-A.

To make sure I had accurate information, I sent a request for his draft records to the National Archives in St. Louis. The handwritten spreadsheets contained no major surprises—just one detail that I had not foreseen—and they gave me a firmer grasp of the process. I was unexpectedly moved by the signature on his draft card, a neater, more formal version of the signature I remember from my report cards (and tried to imitate).

His first classification came in 1940: I-D, for student deferment. The peacetime Selective Service registration took place during his senior year at the University of Pittsburgh, where he was finishing his degree in chemical engineering. My father's first draft decision was undoubtedly an easy one. It made no sense for him to interrupt his education at this late stage, and besides, the country had not yet gone to war. He had no immediate worry about the draft lottery on October 29, 1940. Secretary of War Stimson, dramatically blindfolded for the occasion, drew the first capsule from a fish tank, and President Roosevelt announced the result: men holding the number 158 would be called first.

158! My number for Vietnam! Just a coincidence, but an eerie one. Perhaps it's my Catholic upbringing, but I can't entirely shake off an irrational investment in "signs" like this one. (Signs, in my private axis for classifying the meaning of events, sit midway between miracles and coincidences. I don't actually believe in the endpoint "miracle," but the other endpoint "coincidence" sometimes gives me pause as well.) It feels as if I have survived another close call, like number 001 missing me by only a few hours. There seems to be something, I don't know, *precarious* about my draft karma. I will try not to let this Ouija Boardy intimation shed any influence as I make my way along the questing path.

When my father graduated from Pitt in June of 1941 and took a job with Standard Oil of New Jersey, he faced another draft decision. I see that his registration did shift briefly to I-A after he graduated; but when he requested deferment for occupation, the local board consented: "Reclassified II-A until 12-18-41." My father earned temporary II-A deferment on the grounds that his job was "necessary to the maintenance of the public health, safety, and interest." Standard Oil had sent a document in support of his application. After the attack on Pearl Harbor, my father's draft status needed to be reevaluated. He again requested deferment, and again Standard Oil sent a supporting letter. This time the board granted him reclassification as II-B, meaning "deferred in war production." He would keep this deferment throughout the war. The only mild surprise in his records was a notice to appear for a physical examination in April of 1944. This came at a time when major invasions were being planned, and the country was running short of available men; in early 1944, President Roosevelt instructed draft boards to tighten deferments. But obviously nothing changed for my father.

There are several things to consider as I evaluate my father's II-B classification. The first is what my mother told me whenever the subject came up. She said that Dad would surely have joined the army, but he was not allowed to: his expertise in petroleum refining made him indispensable as an engineer for Standard Oil. She gave me an impressive title for his status—"Certified Scientific Personnel"—and added that he had been specially chosen to work nights on hush-hush projects related to the war.

As far as I can tell, none of this is true. It strikes me now that she must have felt a little defensive about her husband who had not gone off to war. I can find no evidence of the designation "Certified Scientific Personnel." I have learned from research that many chemical engineers working for industry did indeed enlist, or were drafted. As to the specific role of Standard Oil in the war effort, the evidence is mixed. They participated in the essential production of fuel, and before my father worked for them, Standard Oil helped develop a high-octane blend to help British planes counter the Luftwaffe. Some historians, on the other hand, have criticized Standard Oil for complicity with German interests in the early stages of the war.

Let me reframe the question now, having shed my mother's myths. When America entered the war, were chemical engineers like my father generally expected to enlist and fight, or to stay home and work? Two documents from the American Chemical Society provide useful information. "Utilization of Chemists and Chemical Engineers in World War II," published in 1947, points out that many of these professionals had indeed gone into the military. The document clarifies that chemical engineers either enlisted "because they felt it was their patriotic duty," or they were drafted "because of the attitude assumed by some draft boards."

Another ACS document, published during the early stages of the war, exposes the cultural pressures facing young chemical engineers like my father: "Ten Questions that Students of Chemistry Will Be Asking—and Their Answers." It's clear from this piece that young men working in chemistry were feeling a primary obligation to join the military. Question: "Why should I not go into active military service as soon as possible, when so many of my friends are doing so?" The answer is that chemical industries, which contribute to the overall war effort, also need your service; but the phrasing of the question concedes the palpable social pressures to join your friends and fight. Question: "If I ask for deferment, will I not be considered a 'slacker'?" Answer: "No. . . . If you are convinced that you are best fitted to serve in a technical capacity in production, persevere, no matter what the unenlightened opinions of others may be." These unenlightened opinions must have taken many forms—including, of course, messages about war and manliness delivered by Big Band singers. Even the simplest social interactions had the potential to be awkward for my father. Would a barber bring up the subject during a haircut? A soldier's mother in a grocery line?

Another element to consider in my father's decision has to do with his heritage. His grandfather grew up in German Switzerland and his grandmother in Germany. During World War I, when my father was an infant and his father was in his 20s, anti-German sentiment made life difficult for those still described with a hyphen as German-Americans. Posters vilified monstrous "Huns." German-sounding names were suspicious, speaking German was considered disloyal, and in some places, the teaching of German was prohibited.

My father's parents must have suffered under this war-induced stigma. From what I can piece together, his family assimilated well enough but retained strong connections to German culture. At family gatherings they would sing German folk songs, including "Schnitzelbank." When they came to the chorus—"Oh, du schöne Schnitzelbank"—my father sang what he heard: "Oh, why do we *hit the bumps!*" (He was thinking of car rides in their Model T.) I doubt that my adult father gave much thought to whether his cultural identity was hyphenated. But one of the first things he taught his own kids was how to count in German, and we all sang "O Tannenbaum" at Christmas.

It's conceivable that my father's parents, especially his mother, may have discouraged him from joining the new war against the Germans. She doted on her first-born and did everything she could to see him thrive. My grandparents moved to California in the 1950s to live near him. In the living room of their little house in Hermosa Beach, she hung a framed copy of my father's college transcript, which was full of A's in chemistry. But her other son certainly resisted any such family pressure; and I cannot imagine that my father, a notably self-reliant man, would have let that sort of thing overrule his proper judgment.

I have one more piece of evidence to consider. My brother once shared with me a memory of our father referring to war—war in general, that is, not World War II specifically— as "a stupid thing." I don't know the context in which the subject came up. (My brother died several years ago, or I would ask him.) Is it possible that my father harbored pacifist values that made the difference in his decision?

I am inclined to say no to the question as framed in these terms. I have too many memories of my father that run contrary to pacifist ideals. He admired Eisenhower more than any other public figure. When we watched Walter Cronkite's television documentaries about the war, he added comments about poisonous Nazi ideology. He defended Truman's decision about the atomic bombs; and of course he insisted on defending American policies that shaped the Vietnam War.

In short: my father thought that war was a stupid thing, but he was no pacifist. He chose not to serve in the military, but he supported the goals of the war. As I approach an answer to my primary question—why didn't my father go off to war like the other men?—I have to face up to the least attractive hypothesis: that he was a "chickenhawk." The chickenhawk label most damningly includes those who found less than honorable means to steer clear of the draft, like several members of recent American administrations. Donald Trump, for example, avoided military service because his doctor flagged him for what seems a minor foot problem; many have assumed that the doctor exaggerated the severity of his condition as a favor to Trump's father.

My father's case differs from Trump's and the other most egregious examples of chickenhawks in one obvious way: his deferment was honorable. He did not try to deceive anyone, nor did he receive any special favors. He simply applied and was processed through normal channels. When some other chemical engineers did not receive deferments, that happened because their local draft boards either interpreted the law's provisions differently, or faced different contingencies related to their area's draft needs or an engineer's specific job.

There remains another layer to the question, however—something more difficult to probe. Could fear have played a part in my father's decision? Perhaps even a decisive part, as he elected, unlike many of his peer engineers, to stay home?

I'm sure no one ever asked him. And it's possible he never raised the risky question with himself. He was pretty adept at managing the psycho-mechanics of everyday life; I can imagine him engineering a lifelong repression of this particular introspective dagger. As his son, of course, I want to argue that he was no coward. As an essayist seeking truth, I have to confess that I cannot be absolutely certain. But it seems most likely to me that fear played no role or only a negligible role in his decision.

Nothing my father ever did or said leads me to believe he had a cowardly streak. He certainly wasn't the sort of man who enjoyed conflict and sought out occasions to prove his courage to everyone. I've known my share of those. I have only one memory of a moment that included an element of conspicuous physical courage. Just as we finished dinner one night, when I was nine, a woman told us that her dangerous estranged husband had been seen in our backyard. My father took out my Little League baseball bat—the only weapon in our house—and went into the backyard to look around. I remember feeling more excited than afraid.

As I reflect on my father, it is not so much physical courage, but a different sort of courage that comes to mind. As I have suggested, there must have been many potentially embarrassing moments in the 1940s for a strapping young man who was not in the military. I know from watching him over the years, however, that he had a remarkable ability to resist social pressure. He once told his son, who lacked the same ability, that embarrassment was nothing more than a state of mind; it was something that could be overcome with reason and self-confidence. He had a kind of courage that enabled him to do what he thought was right, whatever others might think.

My father was no pacifist, but he considered war "a stupid thing." This remark seems to offer the best clue in my quest for closure. My father had two preeminent qualities. I might call them virtues, but both of these bring liabilities as well as benefits in the conduct of life. One quality is stoic self-control (as evidenced by his defenses against embarrassment, described above). The other is a version of pragmatism. It is this pragmatic quality that best elucidates his comment about war.

My pragmatic father certainly understood why countries end up fighting. But war disgusted him. The slaughter and degradations of war went against everything he believed was sensible. In his own micro-world of stoic stamina, he resolved disputes with compromise and answered challenges with patience. When he went out to our backyard with my baseball bat to look for an intruder, I don't know what would have happened had the man appeared and provoked a confrontation; I cannot imagine my father actually swinging a bat with those steelworker forearms at someone's head.

My father was not the kind of idealist who could object conscientiously as a pacifist. Nor was he the kind of idealist whose patriotic enthusiasm trumped all other motives. Faced with a decision to fight in World War II or stay home and work as a chemical engineer, my pragmatic father likely reasoned along these lines:

He would have shrugged off Kant's categorical imperative. It didn't matter what would happen if all American men acted as he did, because, as a practical matter, they wouldn't.

It now occurs to me, as I reflect on my father's decision about World War II, that I unconsciously imitated his pragmatism back in 1971. I chose neither the countercultural idealism of applying as a conscientiously objecting pacifist, nor the patriotic idealism of joining others in sacrifice no matter the cause. I simply waited to see how the lots fell.

This'll Be the Day

Steve Brisendine

Driving past Clear Lake, Iowa beneath a
cloud-broken May sky, alt-country from

the 1990s suiting this Wednesday morning
drive time and the view from Interstate 35,

and the music segues from the Handsome
Family to Vic Chesnutt, from a sad croon of
Anything to feel weightless again

to a languid half-drawl about
the gravity of the situation ...

the music didn't die on that cold February
night, but it picked up some scars that
still won't heal; can't blame it for hiding
them behind a wink and a gallows-grin.

Leaves on Water

Andrew Graber

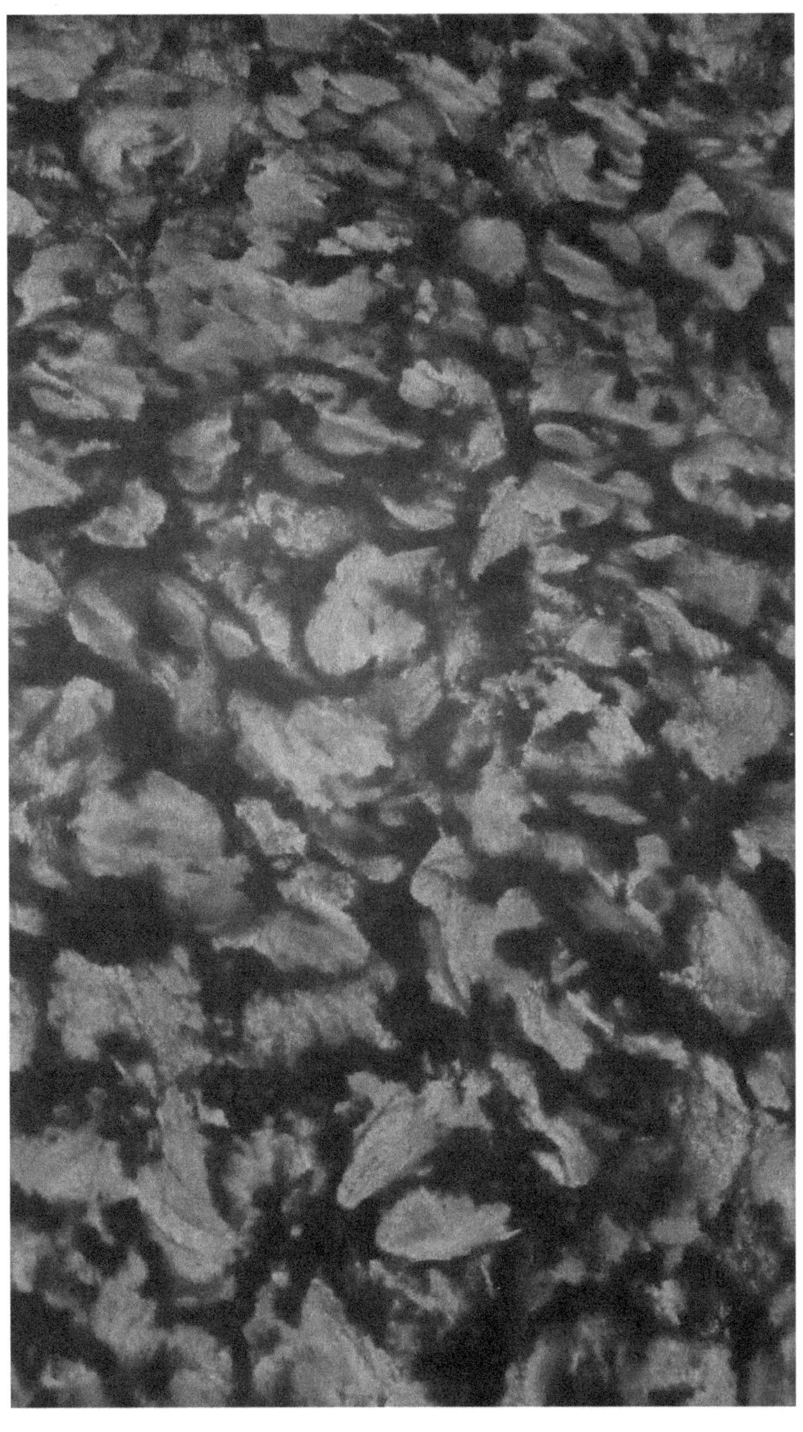

Lucid Dreaming

Miriam Manglani

Let me back in again.
I'll stay asleep,
let you play out as you should,
unfurl your raw self like a sapling
in the fertile field of my mind.

So I can somersault in the clouds again,
weightless, like a dandelion seed,
leap from roof tops to the stars,
slide down the crescent moon
into silvery darkness.

Let me back in again,
and then open yourself
to me like a waiting lover,
cocoon me in your invisible net,
mesmerized and paralyzed,
drunk with the illusion
of freedom in my wildest dreams.

Ebbets Field Bounce

Glenn Moss

If my father had followed his natural strengths, he would have become a high school coach or an instructor at a Fred Astaire studio. Both linked by a rolling grace in his walk, either journey likely would have resulted in a happier man. Instead, perhaps pushed by the macro events of Depression and war, he became a diminished Arthur Miller salesman of women's shoes and a dreamer of deals with other men who found themselves in apartments that were too small and frustrations that grew too large.

One way my father tried to maintain connection with his lost self was to have me accompany him on Sunday mornings for games of handball or boxball. Classic games of Brooklyn that allowed him to move and react in ways that bending down to fit a middle-aged woman's foot in a pump did not.

An essential part of this connection was my contribution…to lose and be the non-athletic kid I was told I was, book smart maybe but having "the common sense of a wet rag". My awkward lunges and misses, hitting the ball outside the lines of the designated concrete slab or not hitting the handball with enough force to reach the wall, both defined me and him. My misses were his hits; my losing was his win. For all the consequences that would flow from this, on a Sunday morning in Spring or Fall it was our time and I saw my father differently, diving into himself in a way that left regret in its wake, but the splash of memory let him make it through the week.

How I made it through my week was not a subject of interest. Encased behind my thick black glasses and stutter born from the pressures of regret and anger that broke the words on my tongue, I was the small pot for the family's boil. Each morning, I would walk to school where my sweating inability to speak oiled the friction of others discovery and hormonal twitch. And to be the source of coin, or occasional coat, for the taking. One night, on another solitary walk down Ocean Avenue on early autumn evening, I was relieved of my jacket, and when I made it home a bit scuffed and chilly, nothing was asked or said. When you meet a set of expectations, what is there to say.

One Sunday in 1965 or '66, instead of the Spaldeen or handball, my father picked the basketball. I didn't remember the last time he had and couldn't know then this would be the last. It was a warm July morning and he said we were going over to the Ebbets Field apartments, a housing project representing the quickening changes of the neighborhood. Changes that would soon be wrapped in the term, "white flight", describing the reaction of white middle- and working-class families to the beginnings of poor and working-class Black families moving in. There were a few middle-class Black families, but they had no place to flee to because racism and northern segregation kept them where they were. Whites could find new apartments and homes in Midwood and Sheepshead Bay or Queens and Long Island, but Black families could not. Many of my parent's friends would leave in the next few years, but my parents pretending to be middle-class economically, would be the last.

Ebbets Field, the historic stadium where Jackie Robinson and the Dodgers began to end baseball's segregation. A place representing the hints of the better people we might be and where my father cheered the team, and Jackie too. But the Dodgers left for California and, like almost everyone around him, other changes brought out fears and reactions to those fears. The stadium, torn down by 1960, had been replaced by the Ebbets Field apartments by 1963. Part of the housing project had basketball courts and that's where my father and I headed that morning.

It was early, around 9 AM, and my father probably thought the courts would be empty. He bounced the ball as we walked and talked about Dodgers and Giants, the teams he still followed, and about the upcoming football season. When we crossed Empire Boulevard and approached the project and the courts, they were empty. The gate was open, and we headed to one court, and my father began to do some layups. He would dribble, turn, and pass me the ball, and I would heave it up, clanging it on the rim of the basket.

This went on for about 15 minutes, and then we heard some voices behind us. "Hey man, what you doin' here…this is ours…" Turning, we saw five guys approaching, all looking about 15 or 16. They stopped, just looked, and one came forward and took the basketball from my father's hands, stared at him, started to dribble and passed it to one of the other guys.

The moment of confrontation, challenge and tension extended, my glasses fogged up with sweat and my legs began to shake. My father breathed in deeply and made his decision. He turned to me, said, "Let's go", and we walked towards the gate as the sound of laughter, high fives and a bouncing basketball followed us out.

My father muttered something, I think I heard the word, "element", one of the code words of the time and neighborhood. He told me not to say anything to my mother, he would say we just lost the ball and decided to come home.

We never spoke about it, but I remember thinking something changed or broke in him. It's not that my father had a clear vision for his future; his eyes always seemed to be cast behind. But an extra weight, a thicker layer of cloud entered that day and never left. There were many things that happened in my family we didn't speak about, but this one was something only my father and I shared…and didn't. That morning, I began to realize that we didn't need to speak for my father to teach me lessons both intended and not. How strength and weakness can be confused, how silence can be a grace or a weapon. How being a father is something you need to work at every day. And you still might fail.

My parents never saw it, but those lessons, however buried, weren't forgotten. By the time it was my turn, it took some digging, sweat and cursing to uncover and fully bring them into my light and fatherhood. That walk away from Ebbets Field continues, and there's still dirt to be removed, but my hope is my son can carry some of these lessons with him. He has other things to dig for, different lessons from an imperfect dad, but at least they'll be his and not buried so deep.

Healing: Half-Forgotten

Leah Wenger

I hear the familiar clink as I walk through the door
Of course he's not here yet
But I am

And hours later when he does,
Who will it really be?
It's the fuse I'm afraid of
Will I be lucky today and catch the long one?

Now I see -
If I don't bring up my concern,
It won't be hurled back at me

But instead it sits and rots
On the pile of half-forgotten stories
And the foul stench has seeped into my soul

Papercut Sunflower

Izzy Lippincott

Voiceover

Amaka Chime

It isn't easy to let the children go
try it: you'll discover the years in between,
the first step, the new formula
spewing out of toothless gums,
overgrown clothes that you find difficult to
giveaway
the tiny fingers rounding off your thumb to the
nearest zero,

from time to time, you feel the presence and
absence, noises above, the running of water,
breakfast for three, two, none, dirty dishes from recollection,
the stale bathroom, the tragedy of empty, sterile places
once dedicated to laughter and now moth
photos falling off the walls
falling because their water is drying.

How do parents survive when tears
harden into the crust of eyeballs?

picking up falling leaves,
bending, bones give way
as leaves are picked, before they
melt in the dust,
yielding to the weather
the morning dew turns to evening mist,

walking forward is looking back
it gets better when you move up
then the memory storage becomes clearer
being cautious with joy is a refund on pain
the more you receive loss is patient,

(stanza break)

the children become their dreams or favorite
nightmares, a bird sings for one to come, or
another to stay away, in all of this
the cradle, as a nest summons
one to withdraw,

stand outside your home; you are inside
sit inside you are in their lives
a machine gun that fires with arms outstretched
the mind a sneaky muscle, weakens by
cutting its vessels,

gather letters in baskets like wombs
till they form a sound
clocking empty spaces with voices in whispers
the secrets are hidden from your deathbed
you are a character in a dream, not yours anymore
so you reverse and move backward

the end comes from the way you came
your fading smile from the battles you lost
outside your skin
looking inside you discover
warranty damage.

Slights

Michael Milburn

1
Stealthy Effect

On the 2020-2022 podcast "Dead Eyes," a journeyman actor named Connor Ratliff analyzes, over thirty hour-long episodes, his firing from the *Band of Brothers* mini-series on the grounds that one of the show's directors, Tom Hanks, said that he had "dead eyes." Ratliff interviews more than fifty guests about their experiences auditioning, getting hired and fired, and working with Tom Hanks, who appears in the final episode to try to recall why he said what he said and what he meant. Having never been the object of a criticism, or a compliment for that matter, that I didn't drill into for its subtext, I empathized with Ratliff's fixation. Over forty plus years of writing, I have hunted for meaning in terse opinions from editors and offhand comments by readers. Offered a specific critique, I worry it like a sore tooth. This picking apart of a word or phrase, especially an ambiguous one, yields both misery and insight, and often illuminates writing other than my own. One bruising rebuff by a literary journal, "We found your poems slight," got me wondering what gives poetry substance or demonstrates its lack.

"Why the hell does everything have to be an epic?" James Wright asked at a reading I attended in college, introducing a short poem he had written. Presumably, he admired William Carlos Williams's "This is Just to Say" and "The Red Wheelbarrow," but still worried that whimsy or brevity could compromise a poet's reputation. It's true that slight hardly inspires optimism as a descriptor of poetry, unlikely to displace "searing," "important," "necessary," or "original" in any blurber's word bank, though it's a common trick of lyric poets to make their works look, sound, or seem negligible, but not be. In addition to the Williams poems mentioned above, with their slender structures and deceptively modest subjects, consider Charles Simic's "Solitude."

> There now, where the first crumb
> Falls from the table
> You think no one hears it
> As it hits the floor
>
> But somewhere already
> The ants are putting on
> Their Quakers' hats
> And setting out to visit you.

In his *Paris Review* interview, Simic recalls the reception for "Solitude" and other early poems about forks and cockroaches: "A couple of editors I showed the poems to were kind of irritated. They said I was just trying to be a smart aleck. More interestingly, they thought these were not worthy subjects." But Simic calls ants "pretty cool" and defends his portrayal ("I've always been curious about these little creatures going their merry way, taking care of business"). He invests his poem with both charm and seriousness, as who hasn't wondered how ants get the word about crumbs or observed the religious solemnity of their rituals. Simic not only refutes the editors' dismissal of them, he demonstrates that a poem's subject, no matter how grand or commonplace, does not determine its substance. In "Cockroach," for example, the speaker's tolerance for the maligned bug accentuates his loneliness.

> This roach is familiar to me.
> We met here and there,
> In the kitchen at midnight,
> And now on my pillow.

Simic isn't the only poet to turn slightness into significance. Walt Whitman's "Song of Myself" ("If you want me again look for me under your boot-soles"); Emily Dickinson's "I heard a Fly buzz – when I died"; Seamus Heaney's "Digging ("Between my finger and my thumb/The squat pen rests./I'll dig with it.") and Wallace Stevens's "Anecdote of the Jar" each elevates its subject through its proximity to the trivial or merely functional.

> I placed a jar in Tennessee,
> And round it was, upon a hill.
> It made the slovenly wilderness
> Surround that hill.
>
> The wilderness rose up to it,
> And sprawled around, no longer wild.

The opening lines of Tennyson's "Ulysses" make no mention of its narrator's glorious past, conjuring it solely through the details of his prosaic present:

> It little profits that an idle king,
> By this still hearth, among these barren crags,
> Match'd with an aged wife, I mete and dole
> Unequal laws unto a savage race,
> That hoard, and sleep, and feed, and know not me.

"Little"; "idle"; "still"; "barren"; "aged"; "unequal"; "savage": each of these adjectives reminds the reader of how things used to be.

As static as a still life, devoid of active verbs or active voice, Robert Lowell's poem "Father's Bedroom" describes the contents of the room and quotes the inscription in a book belonging to its occupant. At first, the writing, like the furnishings, appears to be purely decorative:

> blue threads as thin
> as pen-writing on the bedspread,
> blue dots on the curtains,
> a blue kimono,
> Chinese sandals with blue plush straps

Taken together, however, these details portray a man of refined taste, and, to judge from the quoted inscription, "Robbie from Mother," still subject to maternal attentions. Like Tennyson evoking grandeur by dwelling on its opposite, and Simic finding humanity in the behavior of insects, Lowell uses slightness to stealthy effect—by confining his poem to description, he invites us to underestimate it. In a way, all poems count on our doing this in order to surprise us, as they turn our common language into something original, musical and profound.

The title and opening lines of Philip Larkin's poem "Talking in Bed" conjure an intimate scene, grounded in experience and trust:

> Talking in bed ought to be easiest,
> Lying together there goes back so far,
> An emblem of two people being honest.

The poet provides no description of this particular room and couple, nor does he show them talking—"Yet more and more time passes silently"—reserving his imagery for what's happening beyond the bedroom:

> Outside, the wind's incomplete unrest
> Builds and disperses clouds about the sky,
> And dark towns heap up on the horizon.

By withholding information about the marriage, Larkin ensures that the desolate landscape stands in for it, setting up his ending:

> None of this cares for us. Nothing shows why
> At this unique distance from isolation
>
> It becomes still more difficult to find
> Words at once true and kind,
> Or not untrue and not unkind.

Were the reader not lulled into underestimating the poem's stakes, this final swerve would lose its power to chill.

A poem's length can also create expectations, with long poems signifying ambition and very short ones appearing to demand less of both writer and reader. The size and title of Bill Knott's three-line "Minor Poem," along with the humility of the poem's closing gesture, leave the reader unprepared for its impact.

> The only response
> to a child's grave is
> to lie down before it and play dead

As conclusively as Knott answers Wright's question "Why the hell does everything have to be an epic?" (it doesn't), it's not uncommon for poets and critics to conflate length and achievement. Of all the adjectives that a literary journal used recently to promote a new twenty-page poem based on *The Iliad*—"ambitious," "beautiful," "brutal," "strange," "poignant," "wonderful"—only the first would sound incongruous, though not inaccurate, applied to Knott's diminutive lyric.

If we eliminate length and subject, then what makes a poem matter? What invests Robert Frost's sonnet "Design," about "a dimpled spider, fat and white," with more gravity than Stephen Spender's "The Truly Great." The answer lies in the philosophical precision of Frost's language compared to Spender's hyperbolic abstractions.

> What brought the kindred spider to that height,
> Then steered the white moth thither in the night?
> What but design of darkness to appall?—
> If design govern in a thing so small.
>   from "Design"

> I think continually of those who were truly great.
> Who, from the womb, remembered the soul's history
> Through corridors of light, where the hours are suns,
> Endless and singing.
>   from "The Truly Great"

Another strategy for amplifying slightness is to incorporate it into a greater-than-the-sum-of-its parts whole, as Stevens does in "Thirteen Ways of Looking at a Blackbird." The poem's brief numbered sections have been described by critics as "sketches," "haikus," "word-pictures," "miniatures," and by Stevens himself as "sensations." However one classifies them individually, they make a singular impression in concert. So does the sequence of short songs that concludes the Beatles' *Abbey Road*, especially the last one, "Her Majesty." This twenty-six second ditty, which only made the final edit when an engineer neglected to delete it, gains force from its predecessors and the extended silence before and, as the album ends, after it. Like the white page surrounding Simic's or Knott's short poems, Lydia Davis's four-word story "Index Entry," or the one-sentence chapter in Faulkner's *As I Lay Dying*, this space functions as a kind of frame drawing attention to the art at its center.

Employing slightness as a means of disarming or even misleading readers can backfire if the payoff, the profundity, never arrives. One could say of any haiku-like poem that it is what one makes of it, though asking the reader to share or bear the burden of rooting out meaning risks exposing the poet's failure to accomplish this. Invariably, when very short poems succeed, it's because their brevity serves their effect, as with Ezra Pound's "In a Station of the Metro," as fleeting as the glimpse it describes: "The apparition of these faces in the crowd:/Petals on a wet, black bough." Even without exposition, Pound leaves the reader little room for interpretation, employing word choice ("apparition") and rhythm ("petals on a wet, black bough") to evoke the disembodied anonymity of crowded public places.

Are the qualities that give a poem substance the same as those that make it good? The following descriptions, each written by a different critic, refer to Robert Creeley's fifty-three-word poem "I Know a Man," written in the mid-1950s:

> [A poem about] what we can do against the darkness and chaos of modern life.
> A poem trying to grapple with major questions.
> This poem hints at the condition of humankind in modern times.
> A poem that deals with the problem of finding meaning in contemporary life.
> [A poem] about a world gone out of control.

It's hard to imagine that fifty-three words could express so much; these statements sound more applicable to long poems such as *The Waste Land* or *Paterson*. Paradoxically, the key to the breadth of "I Know a Man" is its compression, the constraints that the poet places on words, lines, and stanzas.

> I Know a Man
>
> As I sd to my
> friend, because I am
> always talking,—John, I
>
> sd, which was not his
> name, the darkness sur-
> rounds us, what
>
> can we do against
> it, or else, shall we &
> why not, buy a goddamn big car,
>
> drive, he sd, for
> christ's sake, look
> out where yr going.

Short poems can take on resonance in the following ways: through aphorism, as in Knott's "Minor Poem"; through imagery, as in "In a Station of the Metro"; through metaphor, as in the Japanese poet Issa's haiku "The snow is melting/and the village is flooded/ with children"; through philosophy, as in Emily Dickinson's "Forever – is composed of Nows –"; and through form, as in e.e. cummings's vertically arranged "l(a." "I Know a Man" employs all of these effects, but none as expressively as form. One need only hear the poem spoken after reading it to appreciate how much it gains on the page.

From a visual perspective, the form of "I Know a Man" appears to constrict its content, with each enjambed line disrupting the words' natural syntax and the abbreviations creating a shorthand that reflects the speaker's urgency. Its herky-jerky movement suits the chatter of someone who "is always talking." Coming from this motor mouth, even the weighty question at the poem's center—"the darkness sur-/rounds us, what//can we do against/it."—looks plausible chopped-up in this way. Similarly, in the last stanza, Creeley employs enjambments, abbreviations, and a lower-case "christ" to invest an ordinary colloquial warning—"for/christ's sake, look/out where yr going"—with a complexity befitting its dual role as a reference to both the road ahead and the existential darkness.

Upon receiving the verdict on my poems, I tried to remember the experiences that had inspired them and my process of trying to render these in an artful way. Was it my material or my treatment of it that underwhelmed? Alas, like all of my attempts to divine meaning from cursory judgments, this one proved futile. Who knew what this person meant or how she defined slightness? I contented myself with investigating its role in literature, and wondering why an editor rejecting her way through a slush pile would add to an already demoralizing refusal a gratuitous, well, slight.

2
Grumpy

John Berryman, "Dream Song #14"

The closest that any of my writing has come to being publicly judged was in a literary journal that reviews other literary journals. Referring to an issue in which my essay about the challenge of viewing art in crowded museums appeared, the reviewer paused just long enough to call it "grumpy." Dismayed at being dispatched in a word, and uncertain of the opinion expressed in that word, I decided not to take it personally and move on. But before moving on I thought about the role of grumpiness in literature, and whether it qualifies as a bad thing, a good thing, or a thing at all.

Few great poems express unqualified joy. One candidate, James Wright's "A Blessing," begins:

> Just off the highway to Rochester, Minnesota,
> Twilight bounds softly forth on the grass.
> And the eyes of those two Indian ponies
> Darken with kindness.
> They have come gladly out of the willows
> To welcome my friend and me.

Wright goes on to describe the affectionate rapport between the horses and the humans, leading to the poem's only hint of unease:

> We step over the barbed wire into the pasture
> Where they have been grazing all day, alone.
> They ripple tensely, they can hardly contain their happiness
> That we have come.
> They bow shyly as wet swans. They love each other.
> There is no loneliness like theirs.

The reference to loneliness stands out in a scene that revels in companionship. Perhaps Wright envies the ponies for not being aware of the solitude that he feels in company, akin to the "aboriginal loneliness of being" that Robert Hass refers to in his essay on Wright's poetry. The line adds mystery and melancholy to an otherwise blissful encounter, which ends in a moment of transcendence:

> Suddenly I realize
> That if I stepped out of my body I would break
> Into blossom.

By darkening "A Blessing," Wright deepens it; by making it less of a prayer, he makes it more of a poem.

Czeslaw Milosz's "Gift" also begins with an idyllic scene:

110

A day so happy.
Fog lifted early, I worked in the garden.
Hummingbirds were stopping over honeysuckle flowers.

In subsequent lines, Milosz continues to report how happy he is, but in terms of his distance from unhappiness, his vocabulary at odds with his state of mind:

There was no thing on earth I wanted to possess.
I knew no one worth my envying him.
Whatever evil I had suffered, I forgot.
To think that once I was the same man did not embarrass me.
In my body I felt no pain.

Instead of noting what he does possess, whom he admires, favors received, his pride and vigor, Milosz portrays his joy as an escape from affliction, and therefore more precious. Only at the end of the poem does he arrive at a position where he can appreciate what's in front of him: "When straightening up, I saw the blue sea and sails."

Probing the underside of one's subject may not be essential to a successful poem, but it offers a way to add complexity through contradiction. Gerard Manley Hopkins's "Pied Beauty," for example, begins by celebrating the Creation:

Glory be to God for dappled things –
    For skies of couple-colour as a brinded cow;
        For rose-moles all in stipple upon trout that swim;

This paean to nature continues for three more lines before incorporating less conventionally appealing items:

All things counter, original, spare, strange;
    Whatever is fickle, freckled (who knows how?)
        With swift, slow; sweet, sour; adazzle, dim;

Shifting his focus from "dappled things" to "things counter," Hopkins reveals that his subject is not Creation, but God's benign view of it in all of its variety, which invests him with a beauty more permanent than that of his works.

He fathers-forth whose beauty is past change:
                Praise him.

Confining these poems to positive images would have limited them. Just as "A Blessing" gets complicated when Wright mentions loneliness, and "Gift" establishes a context for Milosz's joy, "Pied Beauty" extends its definition of beauty to "All things counter, original, spare, strange." Far from making the poems grimmer, these turns increase their positivity. Once one recognizes this strategy, it starts turning up everywhere: in Shakespeare's Sonnet 130 ("My mistress' eyes are nothing like the sun"); in Linda Gregg's "We Manage Most When We Manage Small" ("What things are steadfast? Not the birds"); in W.H. Auden's "Lullaby" ("Lay your sleeping head, my love,/Human on my faithless arm"). The effect works in reverse as well, as when Keats directs his reader to "glut thy sorrow on a morning rose" ("Ode on

Melancholy") or Samuel Taylor Coleridge says of the stars and moon, "I see, not feel, how beautiful they are!" ("Dejection: An Ode").

Even poems that flaunt their negativity can avoid sounding petty. John Berryman's "Dream Song #14 begins:

> Life, friends, is boring. We must not say so.
> After all, the sky flashes, the great sea yearns,
> we ourselves flash and yearn,
> and moreover my mother told me as a boy
> (repeatedly) "Ever to confess you're bored
> means you have no
>
> Inner Resources." I conclude now I have no
> inner resources, because I am heavy bored.

Berryman's comic touches here—the flashing and yearning, the mother's reprimand and the boy's response, "wearily conceded" in one critic's words—temper the speaker's complaint, as does the poem's self-mocking ending:

> and somehow a dog
> has taken itself & its tail considerably away
> into mountains or sea or sky, leaving
> behind: me, wag.

Philip Larkin's "This Be the Verse" contains not a single hopeful sentence, but its singsong tetrameter and rhyme scheme save it from unrelieved cynicism:

> They fuck you up, your mum and dad.
>   They may not mean to, but they do.
> They fill you with the faults they had
>   And add some extra, just for you.

Thanks to his prosody, Larkin's wit comes through even in the poem's final stanza, a free verse version of which would be hard to bear:

> Man hands on misery to man.
>   It deepens like a coastal shelf.
> Get out as early as you can,
>   And don't have any kids yourself.

In "Vers de Societe," Larkin uses grumpiness as a pretext for self-exploration, beginning:

> *My wife and I have asked a crowd of craps*
> *To come and waste their time and ours: perhaps*
> *You'd care to join us?* In a pig's arse, friend.
> Day comes to an end.
> The gas fire breathes, the trees are darkly swayed.
> And so *Dear Warlock-Williams: I'm afraid—*

Were the speaker to continue complaining, the poem would soon grow wearisome. Instead, in stanza two, he brings up a downside to misanthropy ("Funny how hard it is to be alone"), while revealing a positive reason for his dislike of company: his love of solitude. The language grows reverent when it turns from people to nature:

> Just think of all the spare time that has flown
>
> Straight into nothingness by being filled
> With forks and faces, rather than repaid
> Under a lamp, hearing the noise of wind,
> And looking out to see the moon thinned
> To an air-sharpened blade.

But even quiet contemplation comes with drawbacks, and the poem ends with him questioning his self-sufficiency and recanting his opening words:

> Only the young can be alone freely.
> The time is shorter now for company,
> And sitting by a lamp more often brings
> Not peace, but other things.
> Beyond the light stand failure and remorse
> Whispering *Dear Warlock-Williams: Why, of course—*

This reversal belies Larkin's reputation as an unrepentant curmudgeon, borne out in a letter written twenty years prior to "Vers de Societe."

> Seriously, I think it is a grave fault in life that so much time is wasted in social matters.... It's terrible the way we scotch silence & solitude at every turn, quite suicidal.... It isn't as if anything was gained by this social frivolity. It isn't. it's just a waste.

Larkin either mellowed in the intervening decades or arrived at a more ambivalent view through writing the poem.

As the previous examples suggest, unqualified grumpiness serves poets better than their poems. Both William Butler Yeats and Robert Frost claimed to write out of a quarrel, Yeats with himself and Frost with the world, and what is revision but acting on one's dissatisfaction with what one has written? Art forged from discontent doesn't necessarily express that feeling, any more than T.S. Eliot's dismissal of *The Waste Land* as "a grouse against life...just a piece of rhythmical grumbling" accurately characterizes that poem. Eliot's comment sounds more appropriate to the crotchetiness that the reviewer faulted in my essay, which found nothing positive to say about peering through a forest of raised phones in a museum gallery, as much as I meant to do more than just whine.

Originality is being different from oneself, not others.
Philip Larkin

"I've written the same four fucking songs a million times."
Bob Dylan

When my wife began reading her most recent Louise Penny mystery novel, one of nineteen published over seventeen years and featuring the same Quebecois police officer, I wondered at the author's persistence in writing in the same genre about the same protagonist working in the same locale. Given the novels' success and the popularity of their screen adaptations, it's unlikely that Penny has a financial motive for sticking to her formula, so why wouldn't she want to try out different subjects, settings, characters, even styles, like J.K. Rowling taking up crime fiction or James Patterson children's books? My wife expressed little interest in the question, asking me why Penny should find her predictability any less gratifying than her readers do. The idea that an author would enjoy probing deeper into her familiar setting and characters made as much sense to her as the appeal of doing something different did to me.

I feel a similar restlessness on behalf of Elizabeth Strout, whose 2022 novel, *Lucy by the Sea*, features Lucy Barton and her ex-husband William, both of whom appeared in *Oh, William*, published the previous year. They also turn up in *Anything is Possible, My Name is Lucy Barton*, and *Olive Kitteridge*, whose eponymous heroine makes cameo appearances throughout much of Strout's oeuvre. Penny and Strout are hardly the only authors to engage in this practice—Richard Ford, Philip Roth, William Faulkner, Arthur Conan Doyle, and countless other mystery writers come to mind. And while I look forward to reuniting with the Barton/Kitteridge gang as much as my wife loves returning to Penny's fictional village of Three Pines, I worry that recycling settings, characters, and even styles breeds complacency in writers as well as readers. Shouldn't all artists heed Ezra Pound's command to "make it new"?

The newness that Pound calls for has more to do with artistic innovation than subject matter, and many readers appreciate books like Penny's and Strout's for their recurring parts. But there's a comfort to relying on what has worked well in the past that didn't sit well with Pound and his Modernist contemporaries. T.S. Eliot, Virginia Woolf, Samuel Beckett, Pablo Picasso, George Balanchine, Igor Stravinsky, and Louis Armstrong all experimented with styles and structures that revolutionized their respective genres. Poets writing in English who came of age in the mid-twentieth century largely abandoned the formal prosody of their youth for free verse—"seemingly all at once" in one critic's words—on the grounds that the old forms did not fit their new sensibilities or experiences. As a member of the subsequent generation influenced by these elders, I can't shake the feeling that writers, particularly poets, must constantly forge new ground in order to be considered great.

Recently, a friend asked to see my new poems. In her response to one of them, she referred to "that thing you do so well," though whether as a compliment or a criticism I couldn't tell, as whatever I was doing well I had apparently done before. Her comment coincided with my concern about drawing too frequently on the same subject matter, and with my desire to experiment with form. I wanted to write something original, which for most poets is the least likely way of achieving originality. I took my friend's words in the same vein as Pound's advice, which, however bracing, leaves me with a few questions. Should poets always resist the urge to "enumerate old themes," as Yeats put it, or can a poem grounded in convention retain some freshness? For poets such as Philip Larkin, Elizabeth Bishop, Philip Levine, Charles Simic, and Jane Kenyon, writing within established parameters can mask innovation; they renew rather than remake their genre. Defending her dedication to a centuries-old form, Kenyon told an interviewer, "There's nothing remotely modest about trying to write short lyrics in the tradition of Sappho, Keats, and Akhmatova."

What makes a work of art original? No doubt H.W. Janson, the author of my college art history textbook, chose as the image for his frontispiece Picasso's sculpture "Bull's Head," constructed from a worn bicycle seat and handlebars, as a means of raising, if not answering, this question. Picasso is known for his dramatic changes of style, from realism to cubism to surrealism to neo-classicism, though bulls turn up in his drawings and paintings from all of these periods. Among modern poets, Robert Lowell shows a similar changeability. He starts out writing densely metered and rhymed poems:

> The winds' wings beat upon the stones,
> Cousin, and scream for you and the claws rush
> At the sea's throat and wring it in the slush
> Of this old Quaker graveyard where the bones
> Cry out in the long night for the hurt beast
> Bobbing by Ahab's whaleboats in the East.

> from "The Quaker Graveyard in Nantucket," 1947

After Lowell published three books in this vein, Randall Jarrell accused him of "grinding away at all the things he does best," an accusation that he appears to have agreed with. He composes several of the poems in his next book, *Life Studies*, in free verse, writing to Allen Tate that "I think I'm going into new country, and will not be repeating my old tricks."

> His face was putty.
> His blue coat and white trousers
> grew sharper and straighter.
> His coat was a blue jay's tail,
> his trousers were solid cream from the top of the bottle.

> From "My Last Afternoon with Uncle Devereux Winslow," 1959

Lowell's contemporary Adrienne Rich, who also abandoned her early formalism, compared it to asbestos gloves that "allowed me to handle materials I couldn't pick up barehanded." W.H. Auden described the formal, demure poems of Rich's first book, published in 1951 when she was twenty-one, as "neatly and modestly dressed," and Jarrell wrote of her second that "the poet cannot help seeming to us a sort of princess in a fairy tale." Rich bridled at these characterizations, aspiring to be "messily passionate and grand," as she wrote in a letter at the time. The evolution in style in her subsequent books *Snapshots of a Daughter-in-Law* (1963) and *Diving into the Wreck* (1973) reflects both the times she lived in and her desire to confront her experience more directly. She moved away from conventional structures and toward "an unapologetic, even flagrant raggedness," her biographer Hilary Holladay writes. In 1970, Rich left her husband, and six years later came out as a lesbian. "Whenever I remake a song," Yeats wrote, "it is myself that I remake."

A similar impulse drove W.S. Merwin and James Wright toward more intuitive pacings and line breaks in their mid- and late-career work. One senses the freedom they must have felt in leaving iambs and rhymes behind.

April April
Sinks through the sand of names

Days to come
With no stars hidden in them

You that can wait being there.

from "April," by W.S. Merwin

It is the sinking of things.

Flashlights drift over dark trees,
Girls kneel,
An owl's eyelids fall.

from "Rain," by James Wright

After publishing *The Waste Land,* T.S. Eliot predicted that "whatever I do next will be, at least, very different," a promise borne out in the more discursive and philosophical poetry of *Four Quartets.* But this kind of transformation, whether deliberate or inadvertent, did not begin with the Modernists. Impatient with the verbal contrivances of Augustan era poets such as Alexander Pope, William Wordsworth stated his intent "to adopt the very language of men." Pope had "winced" at his predecessor John Donne's irregular rhythms, according to Donne's biographer Kathleen Rundell. Pope "believed that art had rules," Rundell writes, "that poetry was a monovocal exercise; that there was one poetic voice, and we should stick to it." Donne, on the other hand, "did not want to sound like other poets...and invented new words and new forms to try. He created new rhythms in poetry." Rundell portrays him not as striving for originality, but writing in a way that felt natural to him: "It is necessary for each poet to invent his own language....The human soul is so ruthlessly original; the only way to express the distinctive pitch of one's own heart is for each of us to build our own way of using our voice."

Unlike Donne, pre-Modernist revolutionaries such as Whitman and Wordsworth did not go on breaking new ground after their initial innovations. They neither worried about self-imitation nor felt constrained by their established prosody. They did not seek radically new ways to write about new emotions or experiences, a quest that drove Sylvia Plath, in the period leading up to her suicide, to the unprecedented poems of her last book, *Ariel.*

...in the autumn of 1962, [Plath's] marriage ended. The edifice fell, but the poetry came fast and strong. Alone with her two young children in a cold, thatched manor home in rural England, she began writing the poems that would, as she predicted, make her name. While her early, formally intricate poems helped her achieve modest success, these *Ariel* poems—with their speed, daring, and bravado, and their rage against personal and historical oppressions—sounded a new note in postwar poetry....["Daddy"] is Picasso on the verge of cubism.

from *Red Comet*: *The Short Life and Blazing Art of Sylvia Plath* by Heather Clark

Young poets need not worry about repeating themselves, having nothing to repeat. Over time, striving for originality becomes like threading the ever-narrowing eye of a needle, open only to subjects and styles that haven't already passed through it. Another difficulty is distinguishing the stasis of repetition from the progress of honing one's craft or expanding on one's theme. Does success in treating certain subjects in a certain way make any further writing along these lines redundant, or might it yield new perspectives and insights, like Monet re-painting his gardens or Van Gogh himself? Clive James contends that Philip Larkin's poems, despite "a certain predictability of form," are "reinforced or deepened rather than repeated," calling him "more original from poem to poem than almost any modern poet one can think of." And yet the term "Larkinesque" persists to describe his drollery and lugubriousness, a generalization that he agrees with: "We are all on a one way trip to the grave. My usual style."

A clue to this contradiction may lie in Larkin's statement that "Poetry is not like surgery, a technique that can be copied. Every operation the poet performs is unique, and need never be done again." This could be good or bad news for poets concerned about repeating themselves, good if taken to mean that merely writing something new makes it new, and bad in its implication that one should retire one's tricks before they go stale. Auden advised waiting for a cultural revolution comparable to Modernism before changing one's style, but some poets will always be tempted to turn their backs on their strengths. Early in his career, Larkin said in a letter, "I should like to write a different sort of poetry altogether, but when I try I just can't produce even a *bad* poem."

His failure shouldn't surprise us, as he faces the dual challenges of unlearning his technique and becoming unnaturally self-conscious about transcribing his inner voice. "One of the chains around every poet's neck is his own development as a poet," Stanley Kunitz told an interviewer. "Maybe at a certain point he would prefer a fresh start, but the difficulty is that he has already established the condition of his art. To change your style you have to change your life." For Larkin, as for all poets unable to pull off a reinvention worthy of the great re-makers of the past, both the safest and bravest response to writing well is to try to do it again.

4
Sob Stories

"They're not all unhappy," James Wright said toward the end of his reading, a reassurance that many poets might feel obliged to append to a selection of their work. I doubt I was the only listener who assumed that Wright's sad poems would be his best, though some readers fault the genre for its depressing subjects and attitudes. His comment recurred to me years later when an older writer who had offered to look at my poems expressed dismay that they seemed "strucken by grief." She didn't claim to be seeking uplift, but sounded disappointed to find a surfeit of its opposite, and wondered how someone so young could have so much to mourn. I wasn't that young—almost forty—and hadn't suffered many losses, though a few elegies for a friend who had died of AIDS were included in the sampling that she read. My writing, elegiac or not, has always been bleak, which explains my affinity for poems like Wright's. Or perhaps the reverse is true, that these inspire me to mine negative emotions.

Young people often gravitate toward writing poetry as an opportunity to vent, more through complaint than celebration or praise. Eventually, they must learn to turn their venting into art, as only immature poets deem their raw emotions or experiences of interest to readers. "Griefs, not grievances, are the stuff of poetry," Robert Frost wrote. But how to tell these apart? When Gerard Manley Hopkins begins a sonnet "No worst there is none," he might be a teenager reacting to being dumped. Only the syntax hints at a poetic intent, made clearer as the poem proceeds: "Pitched past pitch of grief,/More pangs will, schooled at forepangs, wilder wring." From here on, the reader learns about the poet's state of mind while admiring his expression of it, with the latter proving more compelling than the former: the lines "O the mind, mind has mountains; cliffs of fall/Frightful, sheer, no-man-fathomed" make a simple statement, beautifully. Yet for all of the language's aesthetic appeal, what matters is Hopkins's despair, though whether he simply describes or recreates it in the reader remains unclear.

One of the best-known definitions of poetry comes from William Wordsworth's "Preface to Lyrical Ballads":

> Poetry is the spontaneous overflow of powerful feelings: it takes its origin from emotion recollected in tranquility: the emotion is contemplated till, by a species of reaction, the tranquility gradually disappears, and an emotion, kindred to that which was before the subject of contemplation, is gradually produced, and does itself actually exist in the mind.

In this formulation, the inspired poet seeks to transfer his or her feeling (and presumably its accompanying agitation) into verse. The rest is up to the reader, whose response, Wordsworth writes, "should always be accompanied with an overbalance of pleasure." He cites "Shakespeare's writings, [which] in the most pathetic scenes never act upon us as pathetic, beyond the bounds of pleasure." By this measure, a poet writing about grief must generate "a complex feeling of delight...tempering the painful feeling always found intermingled with powerful descriptions of the deeper passions." To call a poem depressing, then, is to accuse it of insufficient artistry.

At his reading Wright sounded more worried that his subject matter would depress his listeners than that his poems would fail to delight them. But shouldn't any successful work of art, no matter how downbeat, leave the reader exulting in its achievement? "No worst there is none" ends as grimly as it begins, with its speaker craving both sleep and death, but thanks to its rhyme scheme and Hopkins's idiosyncratic "sprung rhythm," its effect is more musical than morbid.

> Nor does long our small
> Durance deal with that steep or deep. Here! creep,
> Wretch, under a comfort serves in a whirlwind: all
> Life death does end and each day dies with sleep.

"No tears in the writer, no tears in the reader," Frost wrote, though weeping as one writes hardly conjures Wordsworthian tranquility. When Chaucer asks his muse to "help me for tendyte/Thise woful vers, that wepen as I wryte!" at the beginning of "Troilus and Crisyede," it's unclear whether the tears come from the poet or the verses. Four of the poem's translations into modern English preserve the lines' ambiguity, while a fifth renders them unequivocally: "these dolorous verses,/that drop like tears from my pen." This interpretation gains support from the poem that one scholar calls "the immediate and principal source of Chaucer's *Troilus*," Bocaccio's *Filostrato,* which asks its reader to "hearken to what my tearful verse will say." Another influence, Boethius's "The Consolation of Philosophy," which Chaucer was translating while writing *Troilus*, attributes the tears to the poet: "Allas I wepyng am constreined to bygynne vers of/sorouful matere...[which] weten my face wiþ verray teers." Why Chaucer chose not to commit to one of these wordings in *Troilus* is a mystery, but the notion of poets venting in verse endures.

As tempting as it is to read a poem about despair as a cry of despair, it's rare for poets to write well while severely depressed. According to her husband Donald Hall, Jane Kenyon needed to achieve distance from her affliction: "When she was mildly depressive, or rising slowly from a debilitating depression, she could write...As she inhabited a fragile comfort, she could work on her poems." Regardless of whether writing contributed to Kenyon's recovery or vice versa, in her poems about depression she frequently frames her suffering as a quest for uplift: "Oh, when am I going to own my own mind again?" she asks in "Travel: After a Death," and her book *The Boat of Quiet Hours* ends "into light all things/must fall, glad to have fallen." These concluding lines from "Depression in Winter" track the speaker's progress from distress to relief.

> I sank with every step up to my knees,
> throwing myself forward with a violence
> of effort, greedy for unhappiness--
> until by accident I found the stone,
> with its secret porch of heat and light,
> where something small could luxuriate, then
> turned back down my path, chastened and calm.

Whether Kenyon actually found a stone and it transformed her mood, or whether the poem completed or even invented that transformation, the reader cannot know. Only the epiphany matters, though if the writing contributed to it, this may explain why Kenyon "wrote poems especially as she climbed out of depression," according to Hall. Of "Having It Out with Melancholy," Hall observes, "It pained her to write this poem, to expose herself, but writing the poem also helped her: It set depression down as she knew it, both depression and its joyful tentative departure. She wanted with this poem to help others who were afflicted." But how much did these benefits depend on Kenyon simply recording her experience, and how much on her turning it into poetry? Is the point at which the reader feels her suffering the same point at which her writing becomes art?

On January 27, 1842, Ralph Waldo Emerson's five-year-old son Waldo died of scarlet fever. Emerson's journal entries for that period "reach the reader heavy and wet with tears," Robert Pogue Harrison writes, and many of them contain lines and phrases that would appear in "Threnody," Emerson's elegy for Waldo published in 1847. In his essay "Literary Grieving: Emerson and the Death of Waldo," Bruce A. Ronda writes that "In the four years between the boy's death and the publication of the poem lie Emerson's personal and intellectual struggle to comprehend the loss, and his effort to translate this loss into art." The attempt begins inauspiciously: a week after the death, Emerson writes to a friend that "I chiefly grieve that I cannot grieve; that this fact takes no more deep hold than other facts." Only in "Threnody," begun four months after Waldo's death, does he prove his biographer Robert Richardson's assertion that "[his] capacity for expression gave him the capacity to mourn."

In much of the poem, Emerson occupies himself with evidence of Waldo's presence:

> The painted sled stands where it stood,
> The kennel by the corded wood,
> The gathered sticks to stanch the wall
> Of the snow-tower, when snow should fall,
> The ominous hole he dug in the sand,
> And childhood's castles built or planned.
> His daily haunts I well discern,
> The poultry yard, the shed, the barn,
> And every inch of garden ground
> Paced by the blessed feet around,
> From the road-side to the brook;
> Whereinto he loved to look.

Finally, this inventory of the boy's favorite places brings Emerson to an acknowledgment of his absence:

> The wintry garden lies unchanged,
> The brook into the stream runs on,
> But the deep-eyed Boy is gone.

The placid tetrameter couplets bear out Ronda's description of "Threnody" as both a personal and a poetic event, a duality that only the best autobiographical poems achieve.

On its own the line "But the deep-eyed boy is gone" would not be enough to manifest Emerson's grief. He has no trouble stating this fact outside of the poem—"My boy, my boy is gone," he writes in a letter the evening of the death, and when nine-year-old Louisa May Alcott arrives to visit her friend the following morning, he tells her, "Child, he is dead"—but struggles to comprehend and accept it. His journal provides little help, allowing him to probe the event without demanding more. Many of the entries are poetical—"And every word came mended from that tongue"; "The boy had his full swing in this world"; "It seems as if I ought to call upon the winds to describe my boy, my fast receding boy"—and one of them anticipates the lines from "Threnody" quoted above—"The loads of gravel on the meadow, the nests in the henhouse and many & many a little visit to the doghouse and to the barn"—but they lack the emotional and formal coherence of a poem.

Only when Emerson begins work on "Threnody" does he need, for his reader's sake if not his own, to articulate his feelings about the loss. And because poetry demands beauty in addition to clarity, his must charm readers with his music as well as move them with his grief. This forces him to process the death more fully than he has in his journals, his letters, his conversations, or even his thoughts. Whereas the tour of Waldo's familiar landscape confronts the reality of the boy's absence, the following lines embody the father's despair, in their keening rhythm the sound of a man falling apart:

> For this losing is true dying;
> This is lordly man's down-lying,
> This his slow but sum reclining,
> Star by star his world resigning.

Philip Larkin writes that "poetry should begin with emotion in the poet, and end with the same emotion in the reader," but it must also divert the reader away from that triggering emotion and toward its representation as art, something that an inexperienced poet may not be able or willing to do. The fact that it took me until my sixties to learn this may explain why the reader who noted my preponderance of sad poems saw this as a symptom of immaturity. In his poem "Many of Our Waters," written when he was almost forty, Wright says, "The kind of poetry I want to write is/The poetry of a grown man," one capable, in Wordsworth's definition, of turning sorrow into an object of joy.

You Fell

Linda M. Crate

i swallowed down
my needs,
became your all you-can-eat buffet;
doted on you in ways you could
or would never dote on me—

think i was trying to
convince myself
this is how love goes,

but love has to be a mutual
admiration and respect;

it is not one person giving their all
while the other simply takes
and takes and takes until the giver
can no longer pour out of their cup—

i recognize that now,
but i see you for what you are
where as i saw you as an angel before;

you may have been angel once
but like lucifer: you fell.

VA Abandoned Stairs

James P. Cooper

Portrait in Sepia

B.P. Mihalich

<table>
<tr><td>1934</td><td>2024</td></tr>
<tr><td>In a field</td><td>I look</td></tr>
<tr><td>she stands</td><td>in the past</td></tr>
<tr><td>Kansas wind in</td><td>her roots</td></tr>
<tr><td>her hair</td><td>now my own</td></tr>
<tr><td>children and farm</td><td>and I am</td></tr>
<tr><td>the fruit of her vine</td><td>my ancestors</td></tr>
<tr><td>surround her</td><td>brought up</td></tr>
<tr><td>a century ago</td><td>in the Kansas wind</td></tr>
<tr><td>she was</td><td>where I stand</td></tr>
</table>

Christmas in Dubai, 2011

Sara R. Sands

"The presents do not wrap themselves," Raga* says, handing me scissors, tape, and three rolls of Christmas-themed wrapping paper. "Thank you for your help."

I look up at her from my newly-designated seat, sprawled out on the Persian silk carpet on the floor. She sits down on the sofa - a very old, expensive antique that cost her a fortune to reupholster in such a fine jacquard. It is beige with dark wood and matches the other beige and dark wood things all set against olive green walls. She leans over, resting her head for a moment on Kynan's shoulder. He is reading a thick book with the enticing title, *Tort Law: Cases, Perspectives, and Problems.*

"Look at my son," she turns to me. "You know how I know he is training to be a lawyer?"

"Because it is two days before Christmas and he is reading about torts instead of making tortes?" I ask.

"No," she says, very serious. "It is the first time that he has a belly," lightly tapping his stomach. "Look at the small belly starting," she says to Kynan. "Just like your father. Has he gotten fatter from all that drinking?"

"Thank you, Mum," he says, snapping shut the book and standing to leave. "Now if you don't mind, I think I'll continue revising in my room."

"Oh, my son, I am so proud of you. You go study, and we will wrap the presents and make a big display under the tree for you. Or perhaps you can come back in a bit and help us? Presents do not wrap themselves."

She sits down cross-legged on the floor with me, forming a human archipelago in a sea of shopping bags from stores with names I either can't pronounce or can't afford. Everybody already knows what they are getting. Earlier that day, Santa the Middleman was cut out. Instead, Raga, Kynan, and I piled into the Jaguar and cruised to the source–the Dubai Mall. Even Duaa, Raga's Filipino maid–a must have for every Dubai family, I'm told–had come with us and picked out her own gift, a new mobile phone with which to call home. Christmas morning would be a perfunctory exercise of unwrapping presents for the sake of snapping feigned surprise photos and reciting the inscriptions on cards.

Not that it matters much to me one way or the other. This is not my holiday, and technically, it isn't Raga's either. After the divorce, Kynan's dad, the Irish Catholic parent, went back to England. She stayed in Dubai to run her marriage counseling and psychology clinic and re-joined the Iranian mosque.

"Can you please pass me the scissors and the jingle bells paper?" she asks. "With the two of us, we'll be done in no time."

* All names have been changed for privacy.

I brought the menorah because I couldn't not bring one. My family had shipped from the U.S. to the U.K. two menorahs. The first one we received was from my grandmother in Phoenix, who had sent us a glass Chanukah menorah ornament from a special Hallmark collection to hang on the tree. The package also included a Christmas tree-shaped guitar that played "Jingle Bell Rock." The two together were a sort of peacemaking exercise – a symbolic gesture to signify her acceptance that I may not marry a Jewish man.

My mother then sent a small travel menorah she purchased from our synagogue gift shop in New Orleans. It had a big Star of David in the middle and blue and white Chanukah candles that were really just birthday candles with different packaging. This is the one I packed.

"It is Chanukah over Christmas this year. Did you know that?"

"No, Mom," I didn't. It was 1 o'clock in the afternoon in London and all I knew was I was hungover and the plate of beans-on-toast in front me, a Kynan favorite, resembled vomit.

"Yes, and do you know how long it has been since a member of our family lit Chanukah candles in the Middle East? In an Arab country?"

"No, Mom. How long?"

"Since your great-grandparents left Syria and moved to America. That's how long. Do you have a menorah? Do you have Chanukah candles? I'll send them."

Kynan had rolled his eyes when he saw me putting them in the suitcase the night before the trip. At passport control, queued up behind an Indian family dressed in saris all the shades of a 64-pack of Crayola crayons, he just about lost his shit over it.

"Between that and your Israeli stamps, you're going to get sent back," he fretted.

"No, I won't," I said. "Money is the common language here, and I guarantee you that Dubai wants my money more than they hate the Jews."

It should not be important, but if we're keeping score, I was right.

"After we had the little-er one," Raga says, referring to her second child, Kynan's middle sister, Mary, "Paul would not let me buy pads for my menstruation. I cut out the bottom of diapers and taped them into my panties."

I'm gliding the scissors across the necks of Rudolph and the gang on the wrapping paper. She is picking up the conversation from the point where she stopped the other night while we were waiting for 30 minutes to try to park at the Gold Souk because I had to see it, we could not *just come back*, and besides, she wanted to ask about some Colombian emeralds.

From my computer speakers, Ella Fitzgerald croons "let it snow." The seagulls outside rise up from the sand in a cloud.

"He served me the papers on Valentine's Day. Did Kynan tell you that?" she asks, referring to the divorce papers from her ex-husband.

"Yes," I nod. "He did."

"It was my first day at chemotherapy. He was my cancer though. It was in my breast and in my home. I got rid of both. I survived both."

"Of course, the bigger one," referring to her first child, Kynan's oldest sister, Katherine, "went with him. As a child, she would take photos of me and poke pins through my eyes. She belongs to her father."

On the mantelpiece at Paul's house in England, there is a picture of his new girlfriend, Carrie. Only for well over a year I didn't know it was Carrie. It looked so much like Raga. I didn't register the difference until, jobless, homeless, and nearly penniless, Paul took us in for the summer. (F)un-employed, I had enough time to stare at the collection of pictures, tchotchkes, and books crammed onto the shelves. It turns out Carrie and Raga come from the same village in Northern Iran, located so close to Azerbaijan that as children they spoke Persian and Azerbaijani as their first and second languages.

"When Kynan came to visit me after I got out of the hospital from my first round of chemo, I came out of the clinic with my head scarf on because I had no hair. I thought I looked okay, but when he saw me there were tears in his eyes."

She is waiting for my response, but I don't have one. I don't have the right one, anyway. She takes that as a sign to continue.

"Every night we would sit on that sofa, and he would read me poems from my favorite Iranian poets and he would stroke my head scarf so I could go to sleep."

Five candles burn in the menorah I lit as the sun was going down. The light of the moon is deflected by the waves.

"I do this," she says, pointing to the tree adorned in red and gold and the gifts and the fine silver, already on the table waiting to be set, "for Kynan, my youngest child, my only good child. My good son."

I take a deep breath. She seems used to this discomfort, like someone who walks around in a hazmat suit all the time.

"I think your daughters miss you," I say. "They admire you greatly. They know you are so brave and so smart, and I think you might find that they are not the same people they were five years ago."

"It cannot be," she says. "That is just what you want to believe."

"I have saved a bottle of wine for the two of you for tomorrow night," Raga tells me. "It is from a patient. He gave it to me last year for Christmas, but I do not drink now that Kynan's father is gone," pausing like a widow remembering. "I hope it will be good. If it is not good, I will be angry. It is so risky for me to even have alcohol."

"I'm sure it will be wonderful," I say.

I wrap Kynan's Massimo Dutti boots, the brown leather belt, and the jacket that is part-gray wool blazer and part-black hoodie. One of those clothing items that looks like you put on two things when you only put on one, and seems like it could be warm, but actually falls short of its intended purpose. Even men sacrifice functionality for fashion.

Raga is writing a card.

"Who's that for?" I ask.

"It is a card to myself. I write one every year," she says

"Every present needs a card," I say, unconvinced by my own platitude.

"Dear Raga," she reads to me. "Thank you for being so strong and for caring for yourself this year. You have been very brave. Keep treating yourself well. Happy Christmas and Happy New Year! With all my love, Raga."

She closes the card, puts it in the envelope, and hands the envelope to me to put on her present. She could not wrap her own gift, for that would defeat the purpose.

"That is a very powerful message," I say, trying to keep my eyes away by focusing on lining up the next box with the wrapping paper. She is crying. Her wedding ring, which she still wears on her left hand, catches the lamp light as she takes a Kleenex and dabs her eyes. I finish wrapping the new cordless phone she bought for herself, place the card under the ribbon, and the box under the tree.

"That's the last of it," I say. "I think I'll go to bed now. Thank you for a lovely day, Raga."

"Yes, thank you for all your help. Have a good sleep, Sara."

I'm throwing away the scraps of paper in the kitchen when I hear someone moving around in the hall. I hope that it is Kynan, but it is not. It is Duaa. I watch her watch the flickering Chanukah candles. The first night I lit the candles and said the prayers in Hebrew, she asked Kynan's mom if I was practicing a cult ceremony. She had never met a Jewish person before. Now, I am told, she thinks they are beautiful and she stops to watch me light them every night.

I watch from the kitchen as the candles burn out entirely, a small whirlpool of white and blue wax stiffening on the foil. The next night I'll find myself here again, surreptitiously pouring half a bottle of the worst wine I'll ever have down the sink while the flames of six candles extinguish one by one.

A ceiling
he didn't know

Craig Kirchner

He snorted what had been described to him as,
"My own recipe, be careful with it, you'll love it."
He didn't remember a taste, or seeing the floor
as it rose to meet his face.

He didn't hear the ambulance, the siren,
or feel the hands as they worked on him,
attempting to determine what caused his collapse,
but mostly struggling with his vitals.

He did see a black screen. No emotion,
just vision, no pain - a small dot of light,
soft yellow, traveling, growing quickly
in a dispassionate, beckoning approach,

nothing else but the warmth, a peace -
which was enveloping, then gone.
He woke looking at a ceiling he didn't know,
his wife and mother at the foot of the bed.

Tests, blood, more tests, nothing wrong.
"We're releasing him, he needs some rest."
The nurse pushed the wheelchair to the entrance,
nobody had much to say, and then,

an EMT standing in the hall, drinking a coffee,
"Good to see you're still here,
we lost you last night for a full coupla minutes,
it was touch and go, but we got you back."

Lake Jeanette

James P. Cooper

Thank God

Craig Kirchner

Turns out this has been done, by everyone.
Dickinson, Hughes, cummins, Rumi -
all thanked the almighty for the sun, moon, stars,
morphed it to an expression, a saying, everyday jargon.
TGIF, thank God the Keurig's working,

there are clean towels, thank God I found the sugar.
To even contemplate doing this
you should have to be down with both concepts.
I'm all about gratitude, could fill pages, go on for days,
soul mate, sex, the condo, the trees.

e.e. cummins mentions that he included the
magnificence of trees. I want to start with desire,
not just arousal, more like the desire to be curious,
to want things other than things, thank God I
need questions answered that don't get asked.

Like about the big Guy, the other concept here,
sitting with the white robe and beard,
sipping a louche absinthe,
with that 'no other before me' attitude,
waiting on gratitude, sacrifice, and prayer.

Like grateful, I'm good with God,
but there's no pronoun, confessional booth,
collections, celibacy, or asks,
there's no Bible selling, or claims that He
speaks to me, about aid to Ukraine and such.

Doesn't need to be thanked, cajoled,
too busy traveling,
pushing the bounds of infinity beyond
our ability to see, to destroy,
to throw bombs at, to kill our young.

Thank God.

My Emotional Escape Space

Dawn Colclasure

Don't get me wrong; I love my husband and kids. My kids, especially, mean the world to me.

But, sometimes, a person just needs a break!

More like, a break from reality. From arguments and bad moods.

That's where my emotional escape space comes in.

My goal was to have some space in our small home that was "mine." Somewhere I could go to just unwind, get back to baseline or try to cool off.

Our one computer, which I use for creative projects, is located in a corner of the family room, where I would often sit and write (or read ebooks saved on it). I grew attached to this space, but it was not "my own" space. It belonged to all of us. In that space was the desk, computer, a table containing candles and all of our gaming gear. All very soothing things to look at, but it didn't give me a way to "calm down" or "center" myself when I needed such an outlet. Even though I was able to do activities I enjoyed in this corner of the room, such as write and read, it was still a "family area." Plus, it wasn't a private area in order to have that amount of undisturbed time that I needed to be the "me" everybody else needed at the time.

I needed a space to call my own.

That finally came about one day, when I started seeing an area of my bedroom as just "my own space."

Sometime last year, I finally found just the right writing desk. Until then, I wrote at the computer, or I used my laptop on the couch or at the kitchen table. I've been writing for over 30 years, yet I didn't have a writing desk in this house we have lived in for over a decade. When I saw the desk that my friend was selling, I knew it was the perfect writing desk for me.

It turned out to be something more than just a writing desk, though. Sure, it had my laptop on it where I could write, books I used for research, and in the drawers were the assorted notes I had for my works-in-progress. But as I spent more time at this desk, I started adding other things to it that are not exactly "tools for the writer." These items were my two favorite scented candles, some rocks I had collected while on many walks, a picture of my kids, artificial flowers my oldest gave to me, a toy dinosaur and a gift given to me by one of my sisters long ago.

These items may not mean anything to a writer, but they mean everything to me as a neurodivergent person with an intellectual disability who also happens to struggle with anxiety, panic disorder, and chronic depression. They are items which help "ground" me whenever I am experiencing emotional overload. Sometimes my emotions just get the better of me, and instead of lashing out or allowing them to make me do things I will later regret, they are the things that I "escape" to instead. They all have sentimental value as well as sensory relief. And they all act as tools for my emotional escape space. Sometimes, my son's dog will join me while I am at my desk, and his presence offers comfort too.

To the left of my desk is a poster of a galaxy in outer space. This is a reminder of my love for astronomy. To my far right is a poster from one of my favorite TV shows, *The X-Files*. I originally got this poster as a reference for a nonfiction book I have been working on at the time, but it's also a reminder of happier times when my husband, who was then my boyfriend, and I were dating and indulging in our love for the show. We still watch it to this day!

But as a part of my emotional escape space, it's just one of the things that can help bring me back from emotional overload and serve as reminders of the reality that I need to find a reset in. The other tools on my desk help provide that reset.

I have since added things to the desk, such as a Halloween decoration of a haunted typewriter and a wolf candle my oldest gave to me. I also decided to keep my exercise mat, kettle ball (a gift from my youngest) and yoga equipment next to the desk, in the event I want or need to exercise in the small free area behind the desk. These extra items add to the ambience of the area and make it more "mine."

Little did I know that when I was setting up this personal space for myself, I was creating something that would provide me with an escape when life just got to be too much.

But this is more than my own personal space in my bedroom. Turns out it's actually something called an "emotional escape space," and I am not alone in creating one.

When I first set up this area at the end of my bed, because it was the only free space I had, I had no idea what emotional escape spaces were. But, apparently, they're a thing. Not only are "emotional escape spaces" a thing, but so are "emotional escape rooms." Some people have set up entire rooms in their homes as "emotional escape rooms," to which they retreated when they were feeling overwhelmed or dealing with sensory overload. These rooms grew in popularity during the early days of the pandemic, when there was too much confusion, fear and uncertainty gripping a majority of the population. With many Americans experiencing job loss, changed work environments and the sickness or death of coworkers, emotional escape rooms provided them with the "escape" they needed from reality. Soon, these rooms and spaces became a haven and "safe spaces" for members of marginalized communities, as well as neurodivergent and disabled individuals who needed specific tools to accommodate their needs.

These rooms are not to be confused with the popular "man caves" or "she sheds" also popular among individuals seeking out their own space. While such environments offer an area of relaxation and enjoyment, emotional escape rooms specifically provide the tools needed for individuals who are dealing with "just too much" of their emotions. These tools – which range from music devices, sensory toys, scented candles, favorite objects and items to abuse or smash – provide the individual with what they need to get back to baseline. In a sense, they are "safe spaces" to escape to when someone just needs to get away from it all and renew themselves. Some emotional escape rooms have a theme ("game room," "reading area" or "music room"), while others are more focused on the diverse needs of an individual.

My friend, Alex Addams, has an emotional escape room in his home, which he calls a "calm room." While his room is still a work-in-progress, as he just moved into his apartment, it already has become a room that has offered him the relaxation and grounding that he needs anytime life gets to be too much. "So far, I have my plants (about 50 or so) set up in there, which creates a really lovely vibe on their own. I'll also have my books, and a large space to do meditation and yoga. I have this light that projects stars and northern lights that will be going in there, as well. It will add the serene lighting and also doubles as a speaker so I can play music as well."

In his last residence, where he had an emotional escape room as well, he shared how it provided him with the escape he needed. "I'd make time to go in there in the morning for a few minutes of calm, and I noticed on those days, it would make a noticeable difference in my mood and level of overwhelm throughout the day. It was also great when I was feeling overwhelmed, because I could go in there and be away from everything. And I had tools like the herbal cleansing or stretching or just sitting next to a plant and candle that could help during those times.”

While not everyone can create a whole room as their “safe space” or for “emotional escape,” there are others who, like me, created their own emotional escape space.

One of my other friends has such a space, and they value it as their own place to find the emotional relief they need.

“The closest I have to a space is in my chair in the living room with my computer on a TV tray table all tucked in and my headphones on,” they explained. “The chair's status as my ‘Personal Escape Space’ is still more or less unofficial though.”

Like me, my friend didn’t see this chair as an “escape space” at the beginning. They noted that it came later. Nowadays, the chair is enough to serve as my friend’s own personal space.

“Sometimes I'll wear a hoodie sweatshirt with the hood up and earbud headphones, it's the best I can do with limited space,” they said. “When I can get the world to leave me alone, I'll listen to ambient music to help drown out more outside noise. Depending on my mood and what emotion needs adjusting, I'll need either minor key or major. Depending on current brain chem balances, I may only need a few minutes to be sociable again, but some days, I need all day.”

Having that space to escape to, or that room to enjoy more relaxation and sensory relief, can be just the medicine we need when we are feeling too overwhelmed, and we aren’t able to find the relief we need elsewhere. The best part about these rooms and spaces is that they give us the specific tools that can help us to ground ourselves again, find a way to de-escalate in a safe and comfortable setting, and do things we enjoy. These rooms and spaces don’t need to be anything fancy or too large – such as me with a desk and my friend with a chair—but they are enough to give us the space that we need to call our own and find a sense of emotional balance.

It All Begins in Water

Noah Hubbell

From the bath, our birth,
until that day that bubble breaks,
we are perfect.

From there, a deluge of error.

To sleep, I try to remember the feeling
by assuming the position of an unborn fetus
and thinking about water.

Warm water in a snowstorm.
A refreshing first sip on a hot day.

When the world seems too sharp
and grand and difficult to understand,
I always return to the ocean,
where my kicks and cries are softened
by the timeless churning
of a greater body.

Super Cell, Pratt, Kansas

Izzy Lippincott

Terrible Heart Rate

Chris Litsey

Panic, panic, panic!
I have to leave!
No time for panic!
Get these tubes out of my arms,
Turn off the alarms,
My blood pressure's fine!
I swear it!

Damn it!
Another test?
Don't you see they have me stressed?
You ask me why my blood pressure's
Sky high!
Why, it's probably the fact I didn't get any
Shut eye last night.

I'm ready to leave; I have work to do,
Mountains of paperwork to sort through!
I passed the stone, why I came,
But I can't pass your exams all the same
Because I am scared to death of doctors and
This serialized white space.
The claustrophobia's made my heart race!
I can't even piss without dragging
My shackles around,
Full of fluids and monitors droning on in
Terrible sounds!

I won't drink as much soda,
I'll watch my salt.
Yes, yes, I know it's all my fault that I came
In screaming anyway, but I can't stay here
One more terrible day. There must be
Something you can do. Pity me.
I just want to sleep it all away.
Please end this extended stay.

Reversals Artworks: Reflecting Upon My Art Process

Jennifer Weigel

She Sings Softly Within
From an original photograph of a Calypso Rose

Photography had always been a big part of my work as a performance artist, but typically in the role of documentation or as a smaller part of a larger conceptual artwork, as seen in my BFA thesis work exploring my childhood migration between parent's houses. I had not really focused on the media in its own right until moving to Boston, MA from St. Louis, MO in 2014. While in Boston, I began photographing the world around me, looking for ways to abstract my existing environment to encourage art viewers to see things anew. I was especially drawn to close up textural studies of tree bark and flowers, as well as public art statues and architecture. I would then print these images on one-of-a-kind materials such as canvas, metal, ceramic, and even slate stone, utilizing varied printing services available online. The accessibility of the i-Phone and availability of print-on-demand services for digital files opened up all sorts of opportunities that had previously been limited to the darkroom environment, and this fueled a more in depth exploration.

I have since continued to incorporate photography into my art practice alongside my jewelry, painting, drawing, writing, and more conceptual projects. Upon moving to Newton, KS in 2017, I began to favor views of the sky, as well as floral details and occasional bark studies, over architecture and public art, though those subjects appeared from time to time. The focus of my photography still centered largely upon abstracting details of my everyday life to encourage art viewers to look at the world around themselves in new and different ways.

COVID had a huge impact on this practice as it forced me to reimagine existing content when cooped up at home, reworking photographs I had already taken rather than photographing new and different subjects out and about. As I began to pursue more publication-based opportunities, I digitally altered pre-existing pictures to further explore how we relate to our surroundings, using PhotoShop to craft new versions.

Kaleidoscope

Original Calypso Rose photograph

In this evolution, I began to consider the role of the image itself as a portal or window into another world, building upon my love of the unknown as it coupled with my newly found love of writing horror stories. These works built upon folk tales, fables, and myths, especially the darker lore involving the fairy kingdom (the ones that steal away babies and replace them with changelings, or the like) or Lovecraftian styled terrors. I sought to take images captured from my everyday life and transform them into glimpses into an alternate reality, another dimension beyond ours that exists outside of our understanding. These unknown visions became simultaneously terrifying and beautiful, both alienating and familiar. The results were somewhat unsettling and yet fascinating.

The process behind crafting these images involved taking a starting image, typically of something naturally occurring like a flower or a tree branch, and then mirroring it to reflect back upon itself. The original image was flipped and folded in transparent layers that conveyed a sort of uneasy symmetry. This sensibility, though pleasing to the eye and our brain's desire to find patterns, offered up a sense of the world that was just a bit too perfect, bespeaking a sort of odd and displaced awkwardness akin to Mark Mothersbaugh's altered found antique photographs from his Beautiful Mutants series. Following is one example of this, built upon a photograph that I took of a thistle plant hidden in grass.

Within the Wilds

Original Thistle photograph

As seen in this piece, "Within the Wilds," sometimes these artworks evolved as more horizontal explorations, considering how an image of most anything, when folded back onto itself in this manner, revealed a structure that we inherently interpret as a sort of face, profile, or figurative focus, like a spirit peering out at us from another time and place. This process provided a means of confounding the viewer's brain to see things that are not present, ghosts that are not there, kind of like a Rorshach Test. But this action and our subsequent reaction also provided a means of reflecting on the times in which we live, as we develop facial-recognition software to isolate and identify individuals in almost any context in which they appear online in the mound of content found therein.

Other photographs were folded back onto themselves multiple times in more of an array or circular motion, creating a sort of inward energy spiral, and undulating pattern that appealed to my more meditative nature. I likened this to a kaleidoscope revealing different mirrored reflections each offering its own unique mandala-like vision, and the result was reminiscent of James Hood's Mesmerica. These explorations involved multiple layers of images placed atop one another, or side-by-side, or both, like strange origami structures. Each version existed a standalone artwork unto itself, and I have even used multiple images in video pieces building upon the transitions between said layers, the resulting movement seemingly breathing in a rhythmic undulating motion, as seen in "Drifting" featured in Woman Made Gallery's Digital Alchemy show. https://womanmade.org/artwork/jennifer-weigel-11/

You can see how some of these works evolved in Spiders from Mars, with the original photograph of ornamental plants reworked through two Tarantula versions, and then finally layered atop one another to create both inward and outward motions within the same overall scene in the final version (title based on David Bowie's Ziggy Stardust).

Spiders from Mars

Original Ornamental Plants photograph

Tarantula 1

Tarantula 2

     My titles for these artworks all related to the overall series theme of Reversals, and then split out different names for individual pieces relating to the moods I wanted to convey. Often these titles inferred mystical and magical beings, such as the Here There Be Elves grouping featuring modified tree photographs, or the Shadowrealm subseries exploring positive and negative spaces through inverted color patterns. Most of the altered floral photographs (as shown here) belonged to the Karma suite, largely because the vivid colors and hidden iconography reminded me of Hindu and Buddhist art. And yet other artworks were titled in reference to pop culture songs or other inspirations. The names for the individual pieces came about after the explorations themselves, as the process determined the outcome and not the idea. This was atypical of much of my art, which is generally more conceptual in nature, based firstly upon the idea that I wished to convey and then considering how. It was nice to work oppositely for a change of pace, responding to the creation of the work rather than designing and crafting art towards a specific end.

What I liked most about these explorations is that there were so many opportunities to evolve new and different images, conveying a huge range of moods and feelings based upon many iterations of the same photograph explored in different combinations. I would tease out a figure or face in one version while simultaneously creating a window, door, or portal to an alien realm in another. I could even digitally collage more images into the mix to further examine the feelings that emerged in the original exploration(s). The experimentation was very playful and exploratory, and the possibilities were truly endless; it was just a matter of folding and unfolding all of the layers.

Allergies

Original Photograph of a Hibiscus

All-Seeing
Digital Collage of Reversals: Allergies
(from a photograph of a hibiscus)
with a Selfie photograph of my eye

Double Rainbow, Pratt, Kansas

Izzy Lippincott

Contributors' Notes

Debra Solomon Baker is a graduate of The University of Michigan and of Harvard Graduate School of Education. The mom of two, Max and Sarah, she has been a middle school teacher in Saint Louis, Missouri for more than twenty years. Baker has had several pieces published, including a few poems, and an essay in *Shark Reef*, titled, "Holy Knight," about a chess-based relationship between her son and a nursing home resident. She also has been a contributing writer for Learning for Justice. She writes to make sense of the world and to try and slow down time. Debra can be found on social media at @debrasbaker.

Steve Brisendine lives, works and remains unbeaten against *The New York Times* crossword in Mission, Kansas. He is the author of five collections of poetry, most recently *full of old books and silence* (Alien Buddha Press, 2024) and *Behind the Wall Cloud of Sleep* (Spartan Press, 2024). His work has appeared in *Modern Haiku, I-70 Review, Flint Hills Review* and other publications and compilations. He has no degrees, one tattoo and a deep and unironic fondness for strip-mall Chinese restaurants. In his spare time, he tries to make himself seem far more interesting than he actually is.

Becca Bullen, a writer and environmentalist from Colorado, discovered her love for writing at a young age. She honed her craft during her undergraduate studies at Point Loma Nazarene University in San Diego, graduating in May 2023. Currently, she works at an environmental nonprofit and spends her free time writing about the world as she observes it. Her poetry and nonfiction work can be found at *The Elpis Pages* and *The Viewpoint*.

Enda Brennan is an itinerant writer originally from coastal New England. He predominantly writes about Irish-Gaelic linguistic heritage and the preservation of indigenous language in diaspora, but also about nature conservation, sustainable land practice, addiction/recovery, and spirituality—all of which he perceives as intersectional subjects. A prior essay, "The Port of New Orleans," was featured in *Another Chicago Magazine* in 2019. They also ran "Dinneen A Day," a lexicography blog exploring selections from Patrick Dinneen's 1904 Irish-English Dictionary. These days Enda resides in another post-industrial sprawlscape of sorts, along the mighty Mississippi River in Memphis, Tennessee. Aside from writing, Enda is also a career waiter, a watercolorist, and keeps a fairly large parrot.

Amaka Chime, is not just a poet but a passionate storyteller, serving as an ambassador for Poets in Nigeria. Her chapbook, which has received critical acclaim, is recommended for Nigerian universities. Her poems are featured in prestigious publications such as *African Literature Today, Journal of the Literary Society of Nigeria, Kalahari Review*, Ravens Quoth Press, and other journals. Amaka is a Wildacres Diversity Scholar and a graduate teaching assistant in creative writing poetry at the Department of English, Illinois State University. Amaka loves to sing and dance when she is not in conversations about folktales or Igbo proverbs.

Kurt Cline (1956-2018) has published five chapbooks and a broadside, and a full-length book of poetry, *Voyage to the Sun*, published in 2008 by Boston Poet Press. His poems have appeared most recently in *Five 2 One*; *Blaze VOX*; *Danse Macabre*; *Mission at 10th*; *Wilderness House Literary Review*; *HuesoLoco*; *Apocrypha and Abstractions*; *Black Scat*; and *Clockwise Cat*. While primarily known for his poetry, Cline also enjoyed a long career as performance artist, theatrical magician and singer-songwriter. The poems included here were written primarily in New York and in Taipei during the last five years of his life, and are forthcoming in his postumous collection, LIMBUS, to be published by <Spot Lit Press> by late autumn, 2024.

Dawn Colclasure is a Deaf writer who lives in Oregon. Her articles, essays, poems and short stories have appeared in several newspapers, anthologies, magazines and E-zines. She is the author and co-author of over four dozen books, among them *365 TIPS FOR WRITERS: Inspiration, Writing Prompts and Beat The Block Tips to Turbo Charge Your Creativity*; *Parenting Pauses: Life as a Deaf Parent*; *On the Wings of Pink Angels: Triumph, Struggle and Courage Against Breast Cancer*; *A Ghost on Every Corner* and *Touched by Fire*, among others. Her websites are at https://dawnsbooks.com/ and https://www.dmcwriter.com/ Her Twitter: @dawncolclasure

Karen Colstrom is a native-born Kansan who grew up on the farm. She has a background in art, graduating from Emporia State University. Karen taught a children's program for 20 years, sharing her love of art. Her current passion is photography on the family farm. Karen's photography is inspired by the beauty of nature.

James P. Cooper is the poetry editor for Choeofpleirn Press, but he has taken photographs since high school. His poetry chapbook, *Listening for Low Tide*, won an Honorable Mention in the 2024 Eric Hoffer Book Awards. To Ruth J. Heflin, who pastes up and edits every magazine, including these Contributors' Notes, James is the sun and stars, a poet-extraordinaire, and one heck of a husband. Brownie points to everyone who admits they read this note on the Choeofpleirn Press Facebook wall.

Linda M. Crate (she/her) is a Pennsylvanian writer whose poetry, short stories, articles, and reviews have been published in a myriad of magazines both online and in print. She has twelve published chapbooks, the latest being: *Searching Stained Glass Windows For An Answer* (Alien Buddha Publishing, December 2022).

Jenn Dean holds an MFA from the Bennington Writing Seminars. She's been published in *Salamander*, *Hawaii Pacific Review*, and *The Writer's Chronicle*, among others. Her long-form essay, *The Keepers of the Ghost Bird*, published through *Massachusetts Review's* Working Titles series as an e-book, won the 2018 John Burroughs Nature Essay Award. The essay is anthologized in *When Birds Are Near* (Cornell U. Press). A former member of BirdNote.org's production team, she hosted their tour of the Galapagos. She's working on a nonfiction essay collection called *Letters from the Valley of the Moon*, chronicling aspects of the Snoqualmie Valley.

William Derge's poems have appeared in *Negative Capability*, *The Bridge*, *Artful Dodge*, *Bellingham Review*, and many other publications. He is the winner of the $1000 2010 Knightsbridge Prize. He is a winner of the Rainmaker Prize. He has received honorable mentions in contests sponsored by *The Bridge*, *Sow's Ear*, and *New Millennium*, among others. He has been awarded a grant by the Maryland State Arts Council.

Wayne Glausser is Professor Emeritus of English at DePauw University. During his career at DePauw, he won several teaching awards, including Professor of the Year for the state of Indiana. He has published three books and over 30 essays, on a dizzy variety of topics, from semicolons to psychedelics.

Andrew (Andy) Graber is a self-taught artist who also likes to sing karaoke. Just recently, he took up photography as a hobby. When in the mood, he enjoys writing short poems and fiction. He has been living in one of the beautiful states out west for the past several years in the United States.

Katrina Irene Gould writes in hopes of demonstrating that we can examine our complicated and sometimes troubling human experiences in order to create more compassion for our struggles. She has spent thirty fulfilling years as a psychotherapist in Portland, Oregon but her deepest love is still writing. So far this year, she's published in *Literally Stories* and in *Writing in a Woman's Voice*. Her work has appeared in *The Rocky Mountain News*, *YM Magazine*, the Eugene-based *Women's Press*, *The Bend Bulletin*, and in professional journals and local papers exploring how therapy intersects with life, parenting, and women's issues.

John Grey is an Australian poet, US resident, recently published in *New World Writing*, *North Dakota Quarterly*, and *Lost Pilots*. Latest books, *Between Two Fires*, *Covert*, and *Memory Outside The Head*, are available through Amazon. Work upcoming in *California Quarterly*, *Birmingham Arts Journal*, *La Presa*, and *Soul Ink*.

Tammy Higgins has published in *Amulet*, Atlantic Pacific Press, *Conceit*, *Iconoclast*, *The International Library of Poetry and Photography*, *Noble House*, *Out in the Mountains*, *Ultimate Writer*, *Samhain Secrets of Irish Horse Anthologies*, '2019 Best New Emerging Poets of New Hampshire, *Trajectory*, and won a contest sponsored by *The Oak* magazine, 'Barbaric Yawp.. Was included in the US/THEM Wolfsinger Productions *Second Wind*, 'Dear Loneliness Project linktr.ee/dear loneliness, the longest letter to fight loneliness, 290 meters, three football fields or almost 1,000 sheets of A4 paper. Also had three photos in The Connected World 2020 Los Angeles Center of Photography; photo Submission in *Urban*; *Health 360*, *Artimpactinternational*, *The Porta Potte*. Also in *Typehouse*, *Carolina Muse*, and *Anti-Heroin Chic*.

A Master of Science and a lover of art, **Noah Hubbell** is an insomniac poet from Denver, Colorado. He has been published as a music journalist in *LA Weekly*, *The Village Voice*, *Dallas Observer*, *Denver Westword*, and *Riverfront Times*; as a medical researcher in the *Journal of Neurosurgery: Pediatrics* and the *Journal of*

Trauma and Acute Care Surgery; and as a poet in *Written Tales*. He finds joy in philosophy and comfort in simple living. He currently resides in Thornton, Colorado, with his girlfriend, Claire, and their yellow Labrador retriever, Pal.

Victoria James is a high school English and Creative Writing teacher. She was awarded a Masters of Science in Secondary Education and a Masters of the Arts in Literature from Pitt State University. Victoria is currently a reader for *Emerald City Literary Magazine* and *Cow Creek Review* while working on her Creative Writing emphasis at Pittsburg State University. Her fiction appears in *Coneflower Café*, Spring 2023 and *Cow Creek Review 2024*. Her poetry appears in *Cow Creek Review's 2023 and 2024 volume, Empyrean Literary Magazine's Volume 6 and Volume 8, Mindful Phoenix's Volume I: The Coping Day to Day*, and *1134's The Archivist*.

Craig Kirchner is retired and thinks of poetry as hobo art. He loves storytelling and the aesthetics of the paper and pen. He has had two poems nominated for the Pushcart, and has a book of poetry, *Roomful of Navels*. He houses 500 books in his office and about 400 poems in a folder on a laptop. These words tend to keep him straight. After a writing hiatus he was recently published in Poetry Quarterly, *Decadent Review, New World Writing, WordSwell, Vine Leaf Press, Hamilton Stone Review, Unlikely Stories, Young Ravens, Writers Resist* and *The Main Street Rag* among others.

Mark Lewandowski is the author of the story collection, *Halibut Rodeo*. His essays, stories and scripts have appeared in many literary journals and anthologies and have been listed as "Notable" in The Best American Travel Writing, The Best American Nonrequired Reading and The Best American Essays. His work has also received numerous Best of the Net and Pushcart nominations. Currently, he is a Professor of English at Indiana State University.

Izzy Lippincott is a semi-retired college professor who unwinds from teaching by driving the backroads of Kansas to take photos.

Chris Litsey is a teacher, aspiring poet, and former editor of Indiana University Purdue University Columbus's literary magazine, *Talking Leaves*, where you can find a few of his published works. He is a father and a lover of reading, writing, getting tattooed, and exploring museums. He lives in Muncie, Indiana, where he teaches and writes.

Native New Yorker and Elgin Award winner **LindaAnn LoSchiavo** (she/her) is a four-time nominee for The Pushcart Prize. Her writing has also been nominated for Best of the Net, Balcones Poetry Prize, Quill and Ink, Firecracker Award, an Ippy, the Rhysling Award, and Dwarf Stars. Her poetry placed as a finalist in Thirty West Publishing's "Fresh Start Contest" and in the 8th annual Stephen DiBiase contest. She is a member of the British Fantasy Society, HWA, SFPA, and The Dramatists Guild. Current books: *Messengers of the Macabre: Hallowe'en Poems, Vampire Ventures, Always Haunted: Hallowe'en Poems"* [2024], *Apprenticed to the Night* [2024], and *Felones de Se: Poems about Suicide* [2024].

Dave Malone is a poet and playwright who lives in the Missouri Ozarks. He spent his early childhood in Riley, Kansas, and later graduated from Olathe North High School. He holds degrees from Ottawa University and Indiana State University. A three-time Pushcart nominee, he is the author of eight collections of poetry. Recent work appears in *Science Write Now, Skipjack Review*, and *Delta Poetry Review*. One of his favorite writing projects is his free monthly e-newsletter. More at davemalone.net.

Miriam Manglani lives in Cambridge, Massachusetts with her husband and three children. She graduated with a degree in English from Brandeis University and works full-time as a Technical Training Manager. Her poems have been published in various magazines and journals including *Sparks of Calliope, Red Eft Review, One Art, Glacial Hills Review,* and *Paterson Literary Review*. Her poem, "They've Come," was a finalist for the Beals Prize for Poetry. Her poetry chapbook, *Ordinary Wonders*, was published by Prolific Press.

Brittney Pierce Mihalich teaches writing at Western New England University in Springfield, Massachusetts. She grew up in Kansas and is an MFA candidate at Fairfield University.

Michael Milburn teaches English in New Haven, Connecticut. His essays have appeared in *New England Review, Ploughshares, The Hedgehog Review*, and are forthcoming in *Salmagundi*.

Caryn Mirriam-Goldberg, Ph.D., the 2009-13 Kansas Poet Laureate is the author of 24 books,including *How Time Moves: New & Selected Poems*; *Miriam's Well*, a novel; and *The Sky Begins At Your Feet: A Memoir on Cancer, Community, and Coming Home to the Body*. Founder of Transformative Language Arts, she offers writing workshops, coaching, and collaborative projects. Her poetry has been widely published, including in *Terrain, Half and One, Poets & Writers, Negative Capability, Mockingheart Review, Two Rivers, The New Territory, Louisville Review*, and dozens of other journals.

Glenn Moss is a media lawyer and has been writing poetry and stories since high school. At Binghamton University, he wrote a play for a course in Jacobean Literature, and at Case Western Reserve Law School, he wrote a play for a course in Jurisprudence. Returning to NYC, Glenn writes poetry and stories amidst contracts. Each enriches the other, with contracts benefiting from a bit of poetic dance. Glenn has had poems and stories published in *Ithaca Lit, West Trade Review*, Oddville Press, *Oberon, Foliate Oak Magazine, Illuminations, Qu, 34th Parallel, Harbinger's Asylum, Trolley Magazine, October Hill Magazine*, and *Narrative Northeast*.

Steven Pelcman is a writer of poetry and short stories and a novelist who has been published in many magazines including: *The Windsor Review, The Innisfree Poetry Journal, Fourth River magazine, River Oak Review, Poetry Salzburg Review, The Tulane Review, The Baltimore Review*, and others. He has published books titled: *Like Water to Stone, Where the Leaves Darken, The Confessions of a Dying Man, American Voices*, and *Riverbed*. He has been nominated for three Pushcart Prizes for poetry. Steven has spent the last twenty-four years residing in Germany where he teaches in academia and is a language communications trainer and consultant. "Capturing the voices of humor or pain, making the small moments epic and witnessing the trials and tribulations of the human experience which captures the heart and mind is what drives the work."

Joan Penn lives in NYC and has a professional background in theater, photography and public relations. She has studied with poets Scott Hightower and Jeanne Marie Beaumont among others, and her work has appeared online and in print in *Griffel, High Shelf Press, The Rose in the World, MacQueen's Quinterly, Half and One, The Closed Eye Open*, and in three Moonstone Arts Press anthologies. She was the 3rd place winner in the 2022 Wingless Dreamer contest for the anthology, *Evening, Wine and Poetry*, and a poem and interview are included in *Nature's Embrace*, published by Written Tales in August 2023.

Andrea Reynolds is a high school English teacher from St. Louis who finished her MFA in 2021. She grew up roaming the neighborhoods of St. Louis city, but she enjoys spending her free time visiting family in Linn, Missouri. Her newest joy is a dog named Rigby.

Joel Robbins is a retired English/Journalism teacher, former Peace Corps Volunteer in Azerbaijan and Liberia. He spends his time as a literacy volunteer for immigrants and as a certified Florida Master Naturalist providing interpretation at a state park.

Sara R. Sands, PhD, is an Instructional Associate Professor in Public Administration at the University of Houston. She earned a PhD in Politics & Education at Teachers College, Columbia University and a Master of Philosophy in Education at the University of Cambridge. She studied creative writing at Tulane University, where she completed a B.A. in English and Political Economy, and the New Orleans Center for Creative Arts. Her work has appeared in *American Chordata*, the *Arkansas Review: A Journal of Delta Studies*, and *The Merrimack Review*. She lives in Houston with her husband and a growing collection of houseplants.

Sylvia Sensiper is photographic artist, writer and advocate. Her writing has been published in *Intima* and *Next Avenue* and she has an essay forthcoming in *The Autoethnographer*. She has also contributed to academic journals including *Current Psychology* and *Children and Youth Services Review*. Her photographs were featured in a solo show at the Else Gallery at Sacramento State University and have been included in a number of group exhibitions. Through the nonprofit project MAPS, Sensiper has helped over 130 of California's former foster youth gain admission to graduate school programs.

Gregory Stump, an emeritus professor of linguistics, is a visual artist who currently works in digital media. His series of asemic artworks draws upon his long-standing interest in the graphic representation of language. He has provided cover art for books issued by Cambridge University Press, State Street Press, and Finishing Line Press. He resides in the Kansas City area. About the art: People often encounter text that they recognize as writing but whose words or symbols they cannot read. This is true of preliterate children, second-language learners, archaeologists examining undeciphered inscriptions, travelers to other countries, visitors to a museum's international collection, customers in Asian groceries or restaurants, and so on. One of the inspirations for the asemic artwork in Stump's portfolio is the unique state of mind shared by all of these people: an awareness that something is a text without any ability to read that text—a text whose immediate significance must be a matter of creative conjecture.

Jeffrey Utzinger has a collection of creative non-fiction essays, *The Risk Involved*, forthcoming with April Gloaming Publishing (2024). His work has appeared recently in *Carve Magazine, Floyd County Moonshine,* and *Chiron Review*. He also has essays forthcoming in *Image Journal, Waxing & Waning,* and *Santa Fe Review*. Jeffrey has an M.F.A. in Creative Writing and a PhD in American Literature. He teaches in Austin, and lives in Lockhart, Texas where he keeps chickens, a duck, and a few thousand bees. You may follow him on Instagram.com/swarmseason or jeffreyutzinger.com.

Donna D. Vitucci has been publishing since 1990. She lives in North Carolina, where she enjoys reading and writing, yoga, hiking, cooking and gardening. Dozens of her stories, poems and slices of memoir can be found in print and online. Her work explores the ache and mistake of secrets among family, lovers and friends. Read selected publications, and information about her four novels, at: www.magicmasterminds.com/donnavitucci. She is a member of Alamance Artisans Guild, and her work can be viewed at: Donna D. Vitucci | Alamance Artisans Guild.

Angela Waldie teaches at Mount Royal University in Calgary, Alberta. She recently finished her first poetry collection, entitled *A Single Syllable of Wild*, which is currently seeking a home. She has published poetry in *The Antigonish Review, Event, Freefall, Grain, The Goose, The New Forum, Paperbark Literary Magazine, Prairie Fire*, and various anthologies.

Jennifer Weigel is a multi-disciplinary mixed media conceptual artist. Weigel utilizes a wide range of media to convey her ideas, including assemblage, drawing, fibers, installation, jewelry, painting, performance, photography, sculpture, video and writing. Much of her work touches on themes of beauty, identity (especially gender identity), memory & forgetting, an institutional critique. Weigel's art has been exhibited nationally in all 50 states and has won numerous awards. See her works at Fine Art: https://www.jenniferweigelart.com/; Conceptual Projects: https://www.jenniferweigelprojects.com/; Public Art: https://jenniferweigelpublicart.blogspot.com/; Writing: https://jenniferweigelwords.wordpress.com/.

Buff Whitman-Bradley's poems have appeared in many print and online journals. His new book is *At the Driveway Guitar Sale*: *Poems of Aging, Memory, Mortality*. He podcasts poems on aging at thirdactpoems.podbean.com, and lives with his wife, Cynthia, in northern California.

Leah Wenger is a multifaceted musician, artist and writer based in Baltimore, Maryland, where she received masters degrees in Historical Performance Voice and Musicology from the Peabody Institute. Leah's expressive poetry is inspired by the small moments in life that provide the building blocks for big moments, but often go overlooked, and her unmetered style invites reflection and curiosity. Leah's poetry has been used as worship resources in the Mennonite and United Methodist churches, and has been published in Eastern Mennonite University publications, *The Weathervane*, and *The Phoenix*.

Ads

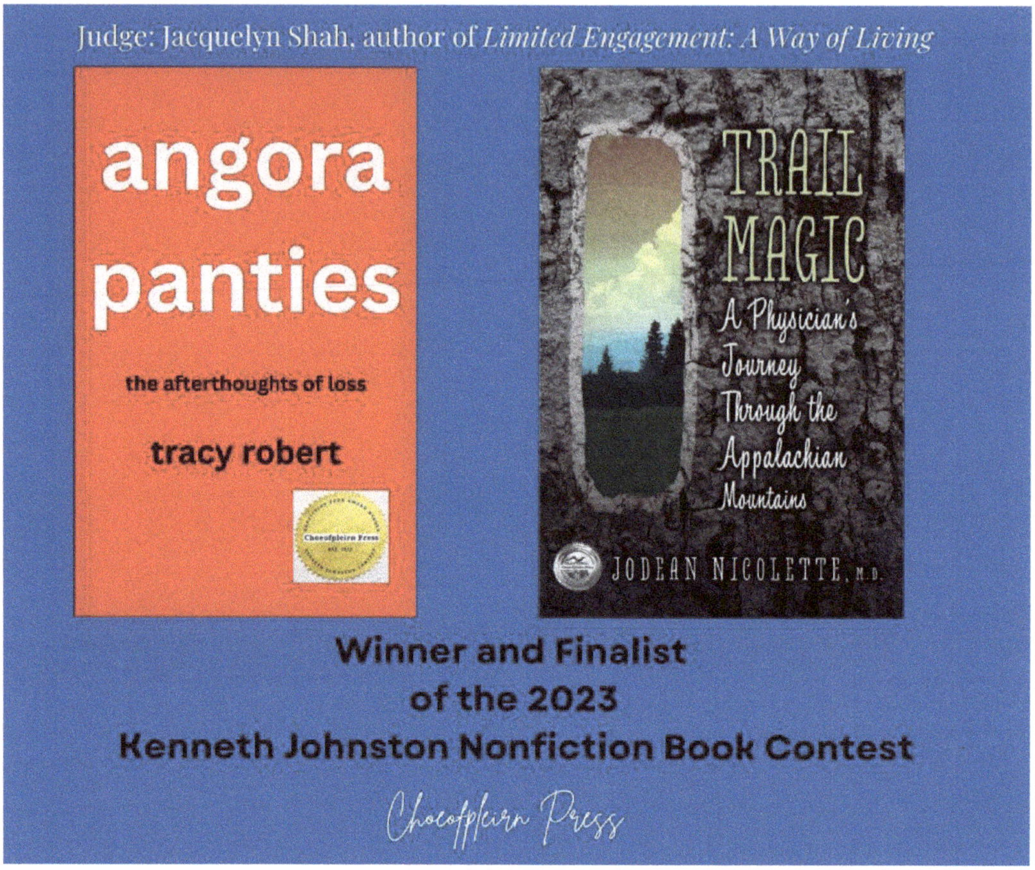

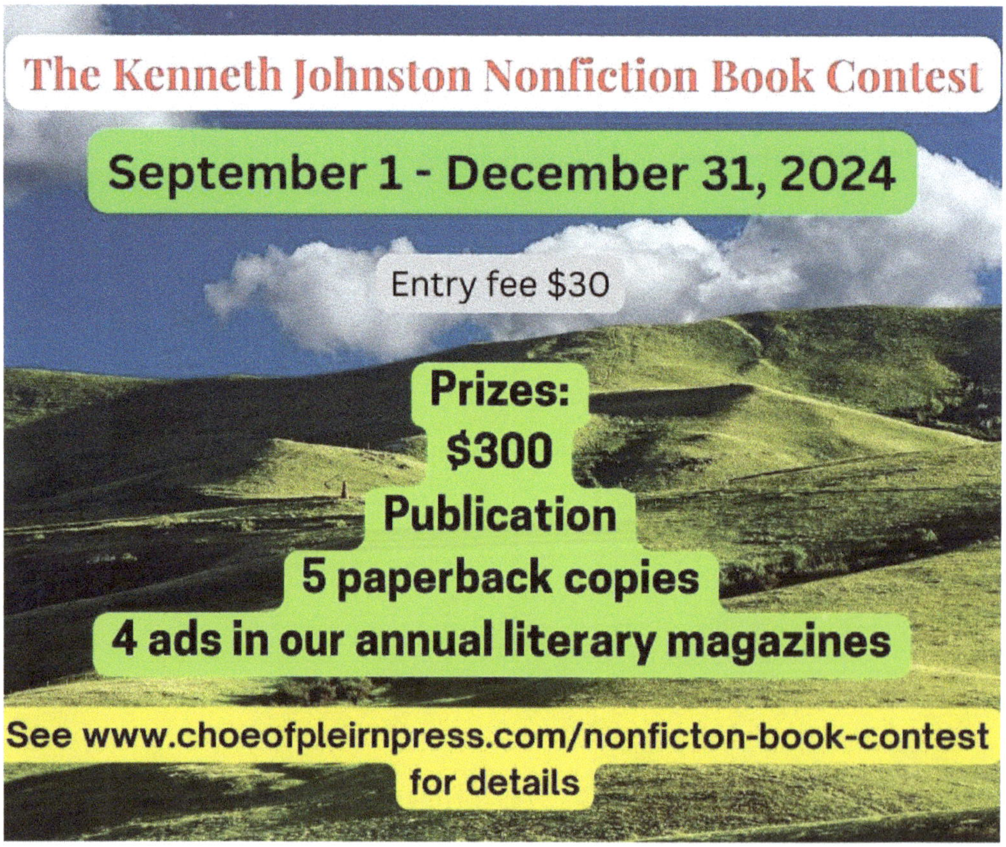

 Fine Art

www.jenniferweigelart.com
www.jenniferweigelprojects.com
jenniferweigelpublicart.blogspot.com
jenniferweigelwords.wordpress.com

151

Available at Amazon and
Choeofpleirn Press

Listening for Low Tide

Too much happens at ground level:
the kids selling candy or delivering
newspapers shortcut through the yard,
the neighbors' dogs blare their alarms
in unison, and teens, shielded by the heartbeat
of their music, speed down the street.

Two stories above the ground,
I welcome the afternoon sunlight
as it stretches across the rug,
my cat moving with it. From the opposite
window, the shadows cast by trees
overspread the ground, the sunlight only
hitting the treetops. Sound waves lap
against the building, the tide at its lowest
each night when the owl in the park
starts to hoot its presence.

Honorable Mention in the
Eric Hoffer Book Awards, 2024

Choeofpleirn Press publishes four annual literary magazines: *Coneflower Cafe* (fiction), *Glacial Hills Review* (nonfiction), *Rushing Thru the Dark* (drama), and the *Best of Choeofpleirn Press*, which shocases winners and finalists of our five creative contests in fiction, nonfiction, drama, poetry, and art. See www.choeofpleirnpress.com for submission details and digital subscriptions.

Jacquelyn Shah's
memoir,
*Limited Engagement:
A Way of Living*,
won first place
in the first annual
Kenneth Johnston
Nonfiction Book Award
in 2022.

Life is a limited
engagement.
Live it to the
fullest
and on your own
terms.